DUBLIN
LITERARY
PUB CRAWL

DUBLIN LITERARY PUB CRAWL

*A guide to the literary pubs of Dublin
and the writers they served*

First published 2008 by
WRITERS' ISLAND
1 Suffolk Street
Dublin 2
www.dublinpubcrawl.com

ISBN 978-0-9559327-0-0

Set in 10.5 on 13 pt MrsEaves by Niall McCormack
Printed by W&G Baird

ACKNOWLEDGEMENTS

I would like to thank the following people for their assistance in the writing of this book: Angie Baxter for editing the text, and for some fine photographs that I have used; Niall McCormack for laying out the book so professionally; Alice Glynn and Derek Cullen in the photographic department of Fáilte Ireland; and Fáilte Ireland for the use of photographs.

I would also like to thank two patient readers: John Hegarty (Tralee, County Kerry) and Derek Reid (The Liberties, Dublin)

A special thanks to Anne, who believed me when I said I was going to write this book.

For Julia and Lucy

CONTENTS

'In Ireland, no man visits where he cannot drink'.

Samuel Johnson

PARIS HAS its café culture – Dublin has its pubs. When you travel to a foreign city these dwelling places help you take a breather, absorb what you have seen and fortify the body for the next leg of your journey. It is just as well that we have so many pubs in Dublin because city breaks can be a tiring business.

This book is designed to help you experience the area around where each pub is located. As a capital city, Dublin has many fine buildings and skillfully laid out streets. Where some buildings are of national importance I have included a separate panel to describe them.

The book is divided into three parts. Each section has been prompted by the many questions I have been asked by visitors:

Fitzwilliam Square

© Failte Ireland

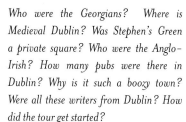

Who were the Georgians? Where is Medieval Dublin? Was Stephen's Green a private square? Who were the Anglo-Irish? How many pubs were there in Dublin? Why is it such a boozy town? Were all these writers from Dublin? How did the tour get started?

The answers to these perennial questions lie in the history of Dublin. Leading visitors around the city has allowed me to observe dramatic changes affecting the city and its pub life.

I have often been asked: 'Have you got a book or the script of the tour?' Broadly speaking, here it is. Luckily there has been a wealth of excellent sources to consult. Special thanks should be given to social historians for recording the memories of publicans and barmen down through the years. These eye witness records are invaluable in establishing the truth about the way things were. Typically, the recall of these elders is accurate and brimming with detail.

Colm Quilligan
July 2008

THE GIFT

It came slowly
Afraid of insufficient self-content,
Or some inherent weakness in itself,
Small and hesitant,
Like children at the top of stairs,
It came through shops, rooms, temples,
Streets, places that were badly-lit,
It was a gift that took me unawares,
And I accepted it.

Brendan Kennelly
Familiar Strangers: New & Selected Poems 1960–2004
(Bloxdale Books, 2004)

INTRODUCTION

There they were as if I had never left them; in their sweet and stately order around the bay — Bray Head, The Sugar Loaf, The Two Rock, The Three Rock, Kippure, the king of them all.

Brendan Behan: *Borstal Boy*

SOME CONSTANTS of the 'fair city' remain. The 'plum blue' hills curve as they stretch down to County Wicklow — the same contours that the Vikings saw when they came 'sniffing the Liffey'. The Irish Sea and the moody Dublin light flirt as elusively now as they did in the ninth century. When the poet Eavan Boland came home to her native city at the beginning of the 1950s, she noticed the 'muddy curve of the Liffey'.

Nowadays, visitors to Dublin will be struck by the number of construction cranes that blot the horizon. From Dun Laoghaire on the southside to Howth on the northside, the city clanks and hoots to the sound of building work. On Behan's return in 1942, Liberty Hall (the first skyscraper for Dublin) had not been built. The city fathers drew a line under its completion in 1965 and thereafter looked on high-rise construction with disfavour. The creators of the new city in Docklands are about to throw out that rule with their plan to build twin towers to gateway Dublin at the mouth of the Liffey. Dublin is to become the Celtic metropolis. To journalist Con Houlihan, though, it is still no more than 'villages tied together'.

Indeed, the centre is quite small, and it was even smaller in James Joyce's time. Leopold Bloom could stop along the street and converse with fair-weather friends and not be drowned out by the noise of passing traffic. In 1904, one could hear the sound of the horse clopping past and the rattle of the tram to Rathmines or Phibsboro. It is still a walking city. Unlike other capital cities, low-density building allows the visitor to study the sky and scudding clouds, and that sudden change of light and mood that Joyce observed when he walked Dublin's streets at the turn of the twentieth century.

Visitors soon come face to face with its Georgian facades and 'days of softness'. They can delight in the muted colours of the city when the sun is hiding behind the clouds, and enjoy its harmonious architecture, and luxurious and extravagant squares, where the brass plates of doctors and lawyers gleam in the morning sunlight.

However, spare a thought for the eighteenth-century visitor to a city with over 2,000 beggars clamouring at the tourist for anything to keep them alive. Well-heeled citizens and ministers (such as Jonathan Swift) would fill their pockets with coins of all values to distribute to worthy causes along their path.

In Joyce's time, the Victorian city was a place of ragged street urchins selling newspapers, pale-faced clerks emerging from gas-lit offices, cabbies huddled over the reins of numerous horse-drawn cabs, trams grinding through badly lit streets, and trolleys swishing past. It was a city of lanterns and fog.

The poet Louis MacNeice saw another side. In his poem *Dublin* he noted how freely the porter ran from the taps. Admiral Nelson was no longer on his column watching the city collapse – far from it now. O'Connell Street is undergoing a multi-million euro facelift. Ireland's most historic boulevard will be transformed – taking it from 'neon classical' back to its neo-classical origins. The city fathers will not get rid of the bullet holes in the columns of the GPO (many

© Fáilte Ireland

tourists still inspect them to be sure). The 'Liberator's' street is to become a European-style avenue. However, they cannot do much about the wind whipping down the street in all seasons, making it one of the coldest boulevards in the world. No wonder the statue of Parnell at the north end wears two overcoats.

Dublin held the mind of writers like MacNeice. He was suspicious of her seedy elegance, 'the glamour of her squalor and the bravado of her talk'. The chatter is still there in many of the pubs. He observed how Dublin is neither Irish nor English. Many others have felt that unease. Historically, the city gave its allegiance to the English Crown from the first Norman conquest in the twelfth century. Dublin was often referred to as 'Young London' or 'the royal city of Ireland'.

By the time of Joyce's hundredth anniversary (1982), important elements of his city were gone. There were no trams. Dublin was without the *Evening Telegraph* and the *Freeman's Journal*. Gaslight was seen only in the Phoenix Park. The slums of the city had vanished but rich and poor were ghettoised in a way that would have surprised have surprised Victorian aristocrats and panhandlers. The city is now divided in a different way – through wealth, education and possessions. The Joneses have moved in next door and so many want to keep up.

Then there are the pubs. Dublin's reputation as a literary city derives partly from the period just after the Second World War. The town was deluged with visitors, all looking for the essentials that they could not get in war-starved Europe – steak, butter and cream. One could be fitted with a tweed suit in a week. Men drank inexpensively. In the misty nostalgia there seemed to be more time – the shout of the sixties had yet to be heard. Even the pints were pulled more slowly and the rhythm of pub life was carefully modulated by the personality of the owner – 'himself' behind the bar.

The poet Patrick Kavanagh was deep into his thirties when he came to the city. In *If ever you go to Dublin Town* he is cautious about how he was viewed by the locals. He was all too aware of the opinion-forming power of the pub – all those 'tongues dipped in vinegar'. Kavanagh advised others to go into some of his favourite watering holes along Baggot Street and counsel the locals about what he was like to know. 'Eccentric' would be the reply. So too is the city. Kavanagh may have taken a leaf out of Swift's book when he asked the reader to

> *Suppose me dead and then suppose*
> *A club assembled at the Rose*
> *Where from discourse of this and that*
> *I grow the subject of their chat*

An early twentieth-century visitor to the city remarked that 'one of the most delightful aspects…is its frugality and lack of ostentation'. In the Dublin of the 'noughties', a city bucking with success, there seems to be no time for the old pub talk. Does everyone sitting around the pub or café table want to be a poet now? Eavan Boland thought so when she went to pubs in the 1960s, but perhaps this is no longer true. Nonetheless, follow the trail around Dublin's pubs and see if you can spot traces of poets and their work.

Kehoe's, South Anne Street

THE PUB TRADITION

In Dublin you are never more than twenty paces from a pint.

J.P. Donleavy

THERE ARE over 800 pubs in Dublin. Walk into one and you will get a feel for how things really are in this 'strumpet city'. The pub has always been the centre of local life. It is the pulse of the neighbourhood. It is where hard news and salacious gossip are chewed over in equal measure. All topics of the day are discussed and dissected. Pronouncements are made on politics and sport, world affairs and, most importantly, the price of the pint. You will find many different characters in pubs: the pub wit, the pub philosopher, the political pundit and the grouser.

The one ingredient that visitors will notice is the atmosphere. That is created by two things: physical appearance and the clientele. Then there is the silence. Sometimes! The pub is a sanctuary or bolthole away from the hectic city. You can retreat there out of the rain. Sitting at the bar allows you to chew the fat with the bar staff, and check the form of the runners and riders at Cheltenham, or discover what 'B' celebrity was in the pub the previous week. Silence is observed as pint drinkers wait for the 'host' to arrive fully formed. The pub is a place for solitary moments. Brendan Behan explained why he went into pubs so often: 'It is because I am a lonely poor bastard'.

The good pub is all about blending (a bit like a good whiskey) – a delicate balance too often destroyed by unsympathetic renovation and the introduction of television and loud music. The interplay between the regular customers with the owner creates a special atmosphere in many pubs. The 'lads' in the pub could become a surrogate family. Friendships and loyalties were often closer here than at home. The owner knew the customers, wrote character references for them when they applied for jobs, and spoke up in court if one of them got into trouble with the law. The publican had the respect of three or four substantial householders; they attested in writing to his sturdy character and sobriety.

The pub was a workingman's club but it was also where men went to get a job – as a docker, a painter, or a bricklayer. They also got paid in the pub at the end of the day. It was important for publicans to have this trade going on – they provided a venue for social intercourse and the tough business of earning a living. Almost every social occasion was, and still is, celebrated by raising a glass. Births, christenings, weddings and wakes have all needed the help of alcoholic beverage.

HOW PUBS STARTED

BARLEY HAS been harvested around the world for over twelve thousand years and historians believe that ale has been brewed for as long. Our Celtic ancestors drank *cuirm* (beer) – made from barley – instead of wine. The ancient Greeks were not impressed: '(it) produces headaches, is a compound of bad juices, and does harm to the muscles'. Patrick (the patron saint of Ireland) was fond of a primitive concoction prepared by his personal brewer. Even Brigid (Ireland's most important female saint) was capable of using miracles to cut short the brewing process of her favourite tipple!

Mead – made from fermented honey and water – was considered the drink of feasting in the banqueting halls around Ireland. It was the brew of a different class in pre-Christian Ireland. According to Brehon law (early Irish law), it was an offence in higher society not to provide food and drink to guests. The king of a *tuath* (kingdom) in Ireland was viewed as suspect if his guests did not leave his castle with the smell of beer on their breaths. One of the most prominent and wealthy citizens in ancient Ireland was the *briugu* (hospitaller), whose status was similar to that of the *file* (poet). The briugu had to keep the supply of beer flowing.

It was the monasteries around Dublin that made a major breakthrough in brewing. Each religious order that arrived in Ireland had a brewer in its ranks. Beer was believed to have a medicinal quality (owing to the vitamin B content). An endless supply of pure water helped the time-rich monk to develop ways of putting the plentiful barley and yeast to good use. The tradition of brewing in the Thomas Street area (now the site of the Guinness brewery) goes back eight hundred years, to the monks of St Thomas' Abbey. Pilgrims stayed in monasteries and were offered food and drink in what were Ireland's first guesthouses. They were to thrive for three centuries, until Henry VIII dissolved the Irish monasteries in 1539.

During the Middle Ages, much of the brewing in Dublin was done by women in the home, and they were equal to men when it came to drinking. Vintners – or wine merchants – were always men. Ale was the beverage at table when water was too dirty to drink and when tea or coffee was not available. The reputation of a house's ale may have led to the establishment of the first 'local'. If a woman got a reputation for brewing, she could sell her ale to the locals. She opened her house to the public. In this way, a trade began. Although women had a monopoly on brewing in Norman times, they were not allowed to sell wine. It was imported mostly through Bristol and La Rochelle and a hefty tax on the tonnage was paid to the English monarch.

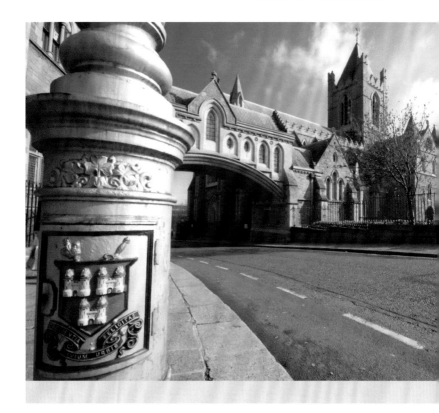

Whole streets in Dublin were soon given over to the production, sale and distribution of beer and ale. Some street names indicate a reputation for alcohol manufacture and imbibing: Winetavern Street (beside Christ Church Cathedral), which dates back to the eleventh century, was occupied mainly by taverns. Indeed, archaeologists have found special tavern tokens from the thirteenth century near Christ Church. These could be exchanged for beer in certain houses. This practice – known as trucking – was outlawed in the nineteenth century.

Whiskey is said to be the 'water of life' (*uisce beatha* in Irish). It was first distilled in Ireland in the twelfth century by monks who had seen the process at first hand on their missionary work in mainland Europe. In the Middle Ages, whiskey was the main tipple at table throughout Ireland. In Dublin, however, ale was more common. Beer and whiskey were both said to have restorative powers and alcohol was commonly used to fight off diseases, particularly cholera.

By the 1600s, Dublin was known as 'the city of the wine flasks'. According to the writer Barnaby Rich, in 1610, the city's profits derived mostly from the sale of ale. The level of public drunkenness, prostitution and riotous behaviour was such that the first Act to Control Intoxicating Liquor was introduced in Ireland in 1635. The government now had a vested interest in increasing the outlets for the sale of liquor, as it received income from the sale of licences to tavern owners. By 1650, Dublin had approximately 1,500 taverns and alehouses. A century later, this figure had risen to 2,300. When Oliver Cromwell, himself the son of a brew master, arrived in Dublin in 1649 (to save Ireland from a Counter Reformation), he banned 'profaning, swearing, drinking and cursing'. By the end of the English Civil War in 1661, a customs and excise tax was introduced in Ireland. Duty on alcohol has been rising ever since.

PUBLIC DRUNKENNESS

BY THE eighteenth century, intoxication was endemic to all social classes in Dublin. Social historians pointed the finger at the easy access to alcohol (the local pub) and its relatively low cost. A man could get drunk for two pence on porter and cheap whiskey. With shift work and part-time employment, men crowded into pubs to look for a job and to get paid for a day's work. Pubs were often packed from early morning to closing time at night.

The tavern was not the only place devoted to the needs of the thirsty poor. As the city became richer, tea and coffee houses became places for political discussion, musical entertainment and games of billiards – and places to do business. By 1750, the population of Dublin had reached 130,000 – almost one-fifth that of London. By

Parliament Square in Trinity College

© Failte Ireland

the end of the century, Dublin had become a town of tattle, taverns and coffee houses; even the vaults of Christ Church were turned into tippling houses. When John Stephens, a young English Jacobite soldier, was billeted in Trinity, he witnessed the drunken, loose atmosphere and a city that was a 'seminary of vice, a living emblem of Sodom'.

By the 1870s, it was reported that arrests for public drunkenness in Dublin exceeded those in London. Many citizens did not have a private dwelling (just a place to sleep), so they gravitated towards a warm, well-run public house. The hospitable nature of pubs led to many customers entering with the express purpose of having 'just the one'. But because of the Victorian 'rounds' system, a 'quiet few drinks' often became a full-on session. Alcohol was cheap. Vanity taught a man to stand his round and he felt that he could not leave until he had done so. The publican did not discourage the practice; it was good for business. When a man could not afford the price of a drink, he was often guaranteed a free pint from his 'butties'. He could enter the local pub without a shilling, then drink and take part in the proceedings, knowing that when he came to the end of the glass, someone would say: 'What are you having?'

SHEBEENS

THE SHEBEEN — from the eighteenth-century Irish *síbín* (meaning 'little mug') — was a place where drink was illegally sold to customers. These drinking houses could be found in tenement rooms on side streets in the slum areas of the city. The quality of the alcohol varied widely, as it was not controlled by breweries or whiskey inspectors. Consequently, the shebeen was hazardous to the health of the customers. It did not take much to set up a shebeen: enough money bought a quantity of porter or whiskey. The shebeen keeper put a sign in the window to attract locals 'in the know'. Word of mouth helped to send a steady stream of customers. Profits were huge because taxes were not paid. The shebeen kept irregular hours and often opened when the licensed public house was closed for business. These houses did a brisk trade all across the slum areas of Dublin in the 1930s and 1940s.

The influence of temperance (*See* PANEL PAGE 68) may well have persuaded Frederick Shaw MP (the Recorder of Dublin) that the city had a sufficient number of pubs and that a new pub could open only when an existing house closed. The resulting stabilisation in the number of Dublin pubs greatly increased their monetary value: a 500% jump between 1858 and 1878. The Recorder's policy became

© Failte Ireland

law when the liquor licensing laws of 1872 and 1902 not only capped the number of pubs but also required a publican to prove himself to be of good moral character to be granted a licence. Arrests for public drunkenness fell from 85,000 in 1870 to just over 15,000 in 1914.

As the value of pubs rose, so did the status of publicans. They had a special pew at church. In some cases, their children became priests or doctors because the publican could afford to send them to private school. In the 1890s, twenty of Dublin's sixty Aldermen had served behind the bar and some of them were later elected to parliament. Politics and the pub were to become inextricably linked right up to this century.

GUINNESS

DURING THE eighteenth century, Dublin became increasingly self confident. The end of the Williamite wars in 1691 heralded a hundred years of peace and prosperity for the city – and a century of coherent town planning and decorative design. It was led by the Anglo-Irish ('a doomed aristocracy', or defined by Brendan Behan as a 'Protestant with a horse'). Those who shaped Dublin at that time were not content to just imitate London. Within a century, they would transform a shabby town of narrow alleys and dirty lanes into a majestically planned city of squares and great public buildings. The people who did it were a mixture of pushy newcomers and Old Irish: those who had made their fortunes out of 'pickled beef and bottled porter'. They were speculators and go-getters who wanted to show off their wealth. They needed a fine house in Dublin for the season. This new trend was taken up by others. Doctors, lawyers, land agents, surveyors, civil servants and business people came to live in the elegant redbrick terraces of Georgian Dublin. They put a brass plate beside their doors to tell the world who they were. The plate was polished (as Sean O'Casey noted) by a Dublin girl in a black dress with a white apron.

By 1759, the consumption of beer and whiskey had grown into a mass market. Arthur Guinness needed to regulate the quality of his ales and bring a new product to the market. He achieved this by roasting barley to create the dark beverage now known as porter. The brewers had by now formed their own guild with St James as its patron. They could exert influence on the city council and would come to wield greater economic power in Dublin life. James's Street was the centre of brewing in Dublin, and a number of public breweries were now supplying a product better than the 'hogges washe' dispensed in the small family alehouses.

By the middle of the eighteenth century, there were about 930 'micro breweries' around Ireland, each producing beer of unreliable strength and quality. Breweries in Dublin were bigger and produced

The Peppercanister Church, Upper Mount Street   © Failte Ireland

beer commercially for the wealthier market. It tended to be of a better quality and therefore more expensive. Inspectors would call to pubs to test the superiority of their products. There was a pecking order too. The Guinness inspector held pole position. Samples would be taken away to test for alcohol strength and colour. If a pub owner adulterated the product, legal proceedings would follow. Whiskey was also inspected for strength and quality. Any publican found to have watered down the house whiskey or stout had to publish an apology to both the producer and his own customers in the newspaper. The apology usually ran along the lines of: 'I (name of licensee) do hereby tender an 'unqualified apology' to you for having sold as your porter an article that was not your genuine porter'.

By the time Guinness was launched on the market in Dublin and London, the term public house was widely used. It became a buzzword to describe the alehouse and the tavern. In 1782, there were 2,000 alehouses, 300 taverns and 1,200 brandy shops in Dublin. By 1797, the population of Dublin had risen to over 280,000 (including the British garrison).

When the Act of Union was passed in 1801, Dublin lost the high spending power of the 'belted Earl'. It was estimated that the 82 peers who lived in Dublin during the season spent more than £600,000 on luxury goods every year. As their numbers dwindled, a new Catholic middle class emerged to demand quality goods and services, food and drink. The number increased when Catholics re-entered Trinity in 1873 and matriculated to the Queen's Colleges of Belfast, Galway and Cork after 1845.

New pubs were built. These were extravagantly decorated to attract respectable customers. (*See* THE GIN PALACE ON PAGE 94) Proximity and convenience were key to a pub's success. Each one built up a regular clientele; trades and professions frequented some pubs more than others. One need look no further than the names over the doors of some Dublin pubs to know who the habitués were: the Wig and Gown, the Dockers, the Ferryman, the Gravediggers. By the nineteenth century, publicans were confident enough to put their own names over the door. This had as much to do with family pride as with placing the pub at the centre of community life. The wooden pictorial sign that swung over the entrance helped uneducated (and perhaps illiterate) customers to recognize their local. Names like the Swan, the Cat & Cage, the Stag's Head and the Bleeding Horse can still be seen. This was an English tradition that was introduced into Ireland in the seventeenth century.

EXCOMMUNICATION

HISTORIANS HAVE often compared the pub to the church in Irish life. Both are confessional, both have a devout following. The priest and the publican had absolute power in their community. Indeed,

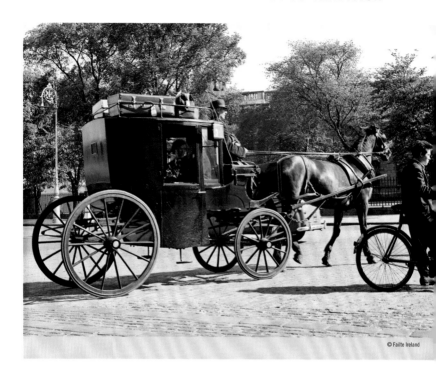

© Failte Ireland

the licensing law of 1872 gave the publican power to refuse service. He was supposed to have 'never a dry cauldron and a welcome to every face'. But he was also entitled to respect and the power to control as if he were in his own house. If a pub was sold, the owner was known to leave a note on the shelf with the names of those who were barred for life for fighting or disorderly behaviour. One would not cross either priest or publican. Being 'barred' from the pub or excommunicated from the church was a fate that all men guarded against. The writer Brendan Behan even used an ecclesiastical phrase when he went on a pub crawl: he was 'doing the stations of the cross'.

Pubs were often fitted out by the same craftsmen who worked on the interiors of churches. Today there is a brisk trade in the purchase of church pews and similar artefacts for use in pubs. In some pubs, the publican had strong religious convictions too (after all, many were from the countryside), handing out holy medals to customers and observing the Angelus prayer at noon and six o'clock in the evening. Some publicans were also known to wear a white star to signal that they did not approve of foul language on their premises. Indeed, in 1825, the Fair Trading Vintners Society advised new licence holders to 'be not too talkative, but speak as much as is necessary to recommend your goods and always observe to keep within the rules of decency'.

The finest pubs had marble counters, old mirrors, mahogany panelling and ornate fittings such as gas lanterns and beautiful chandeliers. All this changed in the 1960s. The modern world marched rudely into pubs and took over. The age of Formica was born. It was led by the crudest developers, content to replace as many facets of Georgian and Victorian architecture as possible. As the value of pubs soared in the Dublin area, the traditional publican sold out to the developer and the investor. It was no longer a way of life for the new owning class. They were not going to live above the pub as many publicans did. The old community-based pub was soon undermined by the huge boozerama. Now it would be about profit, chrome and mahogany fittings - and slick cars driven by the new owners.

THE TRADITIONAL pub has been so successful that foreign visitors have warmed to the idea of importing the intimate look of the Irish pub into major cities around the world. You can order a traditional Irish hostelry from the Irish Pub Company and even specify its style: the cottage pub, the old brewing house, the spirit grocer or the Victorian pub. The result is an Irish pub in almost every sizeable city across Europe and North America.

Tipperary men owned about 50% of the pubs of Dublin. The Cavan publican was a close second. Next came those from Galway. During the land wars of the 1880s, sympathetic magistrates granted pub licences to evicted farmers who had families to feed. It was one reason why pub licences in rural areas outgrew those in Dublin. There was also a strong tradition of men handing a pub on to a relative from the same county. The publican would also hire from

© Failte Ireland

within his own family. This young lad would come to Dublin, serve his time and live with the publican and his family upstairs. The pub might then be handed on to the same relative, keeping the tradition of county allegiance in that pub. It boosted business when the county team came to Dublin to play Gaelic football or hurling.

WOMEN IN PUBS

THE POSITION of women in pubs was always delicate. Traditionally, pubs were the preserve of men. Before the Second World War it was considered unacceptable for a woman to enter a pub. There were good reasons for this. The stink of pipe tobacco combined with the odour of workingmen at the end of a day's labour made pubs filthy places for women to enter. Added to this was the sawdust on the floor to soak up men's spittle and vomit from excessive drinking. These conditions made most women pub-shy. The discomfort was exacerbated by the absence of toilet facilities for them.

There were exceptions to the 'no women' rule. One such person was the revered granny. After rearing a dozen kids, scores of grandchildren and even great grandchildren (like 'Red Magso' in Christy Brown's *Down All the Days*), this formidable woman had earned the right to sit in a pub. Her reputation could not be sullied either. Anyone who crossed her would answer to her extended family. The 'shawlie' street trader also came into the 'early pubs' in the market districts. She would warm up at the open fire and bring a 'sup' back out with her to the stall where she sold fruit and vegetables.

Women brought change to the pub trade. The shrewd publican saw that providing new comforts for a high-spending group — often happier to drink spirits and mixers — was a way of attracting new business. The lounge was added to many pubs. These bright, spacious areas soon caught on, especially in the suburban pub. The first lounge in a Dublin pub appeared in Doran's of Marlborough Street in 1938. The pub was quickly dubbed the 'pros' cathedral' as it was near to the city's only Catholic cathedral and close to the notorious 'Monto' (red light district).

A STORY is told of two *oul' ones* who went into the Pro-Cathedral (near Doran's) to make their confession, having had a few jars in the pub. One of the women fell asleep in the confession box, while waiting for the slide to be pulled back. She woke suddenly and, seeing the priest behind the wire mesh, said: 'Give us two more bottles of stout and would you turn on the f***in' light in the snug' (from *Dublin Pub Life & Lore*).

Women and married couples had gone to hotels like the Shelbourne, the Hibernian and the Gresham for the gilt and extra comfort. Now they found this comfort in a public house. Dubliners were shocked at the new development but it quickly took off. If women could work in factories and earn a living, they had earned the right to go into pubs along with their male counterparts. Technically, a publican could still refuse to serve a woman until the Equal Status Act became law in 2000. Even into the 1990s, the traditional publican was heard to say to a mixed group of revellers: 'Ladies will be served in the lounge'.

For centuries, the spirit grocer pub did allow women to come in to buy groceries in the unlicensed section of the pub. (*See* SPIRIT GROCERS ON PAGE 61) They could also buy 'off-sales' alcohol and sit in the snug. They could be seen smoking a pipe under their shawls (never in public), while male drinkers at the bar noted how they whispered discreetly to each other, like in the 'confession box'.

GREAT DUBLIN snugs (snuggeries): Kehoe's (South Anne Street), the Palace Bar (Fleet Street), Ryan's (Parkgate Street), Toner's and Doheny & Nesbitt's (both in Lower Baggot Street), Slattery's (Rathmines Road), and the Lord Edward (Christchurch Place).

Prostitutes happily acquired customers in a pub, if they were allowed. The playwright Sean O'Casey shocked the nation in Act II of *The Plough and the Stars* — Rosie Redmond, a prostitute, sits at the bar and bemoans the lack of interest in a 'girl's garthers' when customers turn to the holy business of politics.

While the absence of toilets in pubs was a drawback for women, it was also hazardous for the male staff. Very often women would exit the pub and relieve themselves over the cellar grate, to the consternation of the porter standing underneath. One publican in Ringsend claimed to have the first idea for a ladies' toilet: a biscuit tin filled with sawdust as a silencer and placed in the snug!

Although women were not supposed to go into pubs, they could linger at the doorway and catch the publican's eye. He would fill their jug or billycan with porter. Even up to the 1970s, it was common to see women with children waiting outside pubs for their husbands to finish their pints. It was frowned upon for a woman to go into a pub looking for her husband. She had to wait outside and ask someone to call him out instead. He could not be made to look foolish in front of his friends.

Grandmothers would often send children to the pub for a jug of porter or a 'bottle of holy water' (whiskey). This is how the writer Brendan Behan was introduced to alcohol; he was just eight years old. Women looked forward to funeral days because they got a dispensation to enter pubs. They came to drink, laugh and sing the praises of the dead person at a pub wake, and they got time away from the daily drudgery of household chores.

FUNERAL DIRECTING

BEFORE THE advent of motorised ambulances, a publican was allowed to receive a dead body into the cool store room of his pub until it could be examined by the coroner and the cause of death determined. This led to publicans setting up in a new trade: funeral directing.

THE MARKET PUBS

THE SMITHFIELD pub scene has changed beyond all recognition. The area was once packed with pig and cattle salesmen, farriers and corn dealers; it also had three distilleries. In 1665, a monthly horse market was set up in Smithfield. This colourful event gave Travellers a chance to buy and sell horses, pigs, goats, sheep, cattle, hay and straw. Tanglers or middlemen did deals in the pubs; these deals were often closed in the snug. At one time, up to 8,000 head of cattle would be moved through the city on shipping days. Pubs were particularly busy on Thursdays, as pensions were collected at the post office and policemen got paid that day.

IN 1929, a pint of stout cost 1 penny.

Predictably, fighting was common when the horse fair was in full swing. Traveller clans from different parts of the country would square up to each other after a skinful of bad wine. Pubs were full of men dealing in cattle. English buyers of beef were also present and they bought large quantities of whiskey to bring home. The area was 'paved with dust, horse dung and consumptive spits'. Smithfield is now properly paved and lit by designer floodlights and has been transformed into an upmarket enclave of shops, coffee bars and very expensive apartments.

The cattle drovers of Smithfield stayed in the cheap bed and breakfast houses on the North Circular Road, giving them easy access to Smithfield and the docks. They were different to those men who had a trade: bricklayers, plasterers or carpenters. These were skilled labourers who considered themselves to be of a higher class. They went to certain pubs to get a job in the morning and got paid there at the end of the day. The trade union leader James Larkin campaigned against this practice, as very little of the money was brought home to the wives and children. The custom had been proscribed by the Payment of Wages in Public Houses (Prohibition)

Act of 1833. Larkin also changed the unspoken rule of buying one's 'jobbie' (subcontractor) a pint in order to get hired again; it was widely practised until greater union membership raised workers' consciousness about the unfairness of the tradition.

The market pubs had very little in the way of furniture, apart from some stools and narrow tables. The shelf at elbow height was popular, allowing a man to stand, park his pint and have a quiet chat with his friend or co-worker. The scarcity of the furnishings allowed maximum movement and speedy flow through the pub. Business was always brisk at lunchtime and then the publican had an hour off (2.30pm to 3.30pm) to clean up (see THE HOLY HOUR). The 'curate' (young barman) would take a break until 7pm.

THE HOLY HOUR

THIS CHARMING tradition was done away with in 1988. In Dublin and Cork, pubs closed between 2.30pm and 3.30pm (between 2pm and 4pm on Sundays) to give publicans and staff a chance to clear up what were often very messy pubs – particularly in market areas and around the docklands. Publicans welcomed the time off. Floors were swept, glasses washed, ashtrays cleaned, spittoons emptied and fresh sawdust spread on the floor. All this was achieved in an hour while the publican spread out the evening newspaper and checked the runners and riders at Haydock Park or the death notices inside the back page. The closure favoured the insider who, with a nod and a wink from the publican, would be allowed to stay on and drink until the pub reopened an hour later.

The 'holy hour' was important when pubs were workingmen's clubs or places of business in the docks and market areas, but it became a barrier to business for tourists and the changing work patterns in the city.

In the pubs in working class areas, the 'slate' was a godsend. Publicans could not do business without it, although it was technically against the law. The Drink on Credit to Servants Act of 1735 outlawed the serving of alcohol on credit and a publican had no recourse in law if debts were not paid. He would of course bar the man that refused to pay him, and men were frightened of that. They got paid in cash by the day and the week, and the slate was wiped clean on payday.

THE BOOKMAKER (BOOKIE)

BEFORE BETTING shops came to Dublin, there was always a 'turf accountant' in the local pub. Indeed, the first bookies were publicans. But betting 'under the influence' was declared illegal by a number of Acts in the nineteenth century. Street betting was permitted from 1878 but it was made illegal in 1906. According to publicans and barmen, this trade gravitated towards the pub. A book was 'opened' when a large sum of money was deposited with the publican for safe keeping. By law, the only place that cash bets could be made was at a racecourse. In reality, though, the bookie was a regular dealer in busy Dublin pubs – especially on Saturdays and paydays. The whole trade was regulated by the Betting Act of 1926, when the Free State government stepped in to earn much needed revenue from the trade. It allowed betting shops to set up – close to pubs – on side streets and alleys.

PUBS WITHOUT PUBLICANS

The soul of the Dublin pub has been lost to television.

Con Houlihan

AT ONE time it was impossible to cross the city without passing a pub, but the task is easier now. The superpub has taken over the pub trade in the city centre. A pub licence can change hands for about

€100,000 (the price was set at five shillings by the first statute in 1635) but the profit lies in the volume trade after the inevitable makeover. The need to increase sales of drink means that pub space has to quadruple if businesses are to get a return on investments. The superpub has done to the intimate local what supermarkets and out-of-town megastores have done to the small grocer.

Gone are the frosted glass panes that protected the privacy of the pub habitué and added to the calm, confessional atmosphere. Now one can see into almost every pub. Out went the snug and the Victorian partition; in came the chrome stools and plush velvet finish. It is all a far cry from the 1960s, when Dublin was no more than an inward-looking town between two canals, where pubs and cafés burnt peat in the fire and served tea and brown scones. The rhythm of people's conversation was what you heard when you pushed in the door of a Dublin pub. It is an altogether different beat that pulsates now.

Dublin is said to be a city in love with words. You would expect to find this tradition alive and well in the local pub, but only the most gullible visitor would expect to find a boozy Behanesque character regaling those around him in song and apocryphal story. You are unlikely to see a group of young people arguing about street references in *Ulysses* – indeed, many of these have been bulldozed off the map. You would, however, expect to go into a pub to unwind and talk.

In the last twenty years, some of the most renowned city centre pubs have been taken over by developers and knocked down, only to be replaced by a large drinking hall. Synott's (South King Street) – a small pub just across the road from the Gaiety Theatre – was such a place. It hosted performers and show-goers for decades, until the St Stephen's Green Shopping Centre was built. In its place is a sports bar, with a nod to its theatrical origins. For the collection of writers' portraits and memorabilia alone, the pub is worth visiting.

The theme pub is often a vast boozerama, sometimes accommodating over a thousand people at any given time and attracting a certain type of young professional. Many in this age group previously emigrated from Ireland, particularly in the 1980s, and spent their earnings in other countries. That trend has emphatically

McDaid's Pub   © Failte Ireland

reversed since the coming of the 'Celtic Tiger'. In the new century, there is net immigration to Ireland (about 10% of the population are non-nationals). Examples of the new 'swigging parlours' include the Market Bar, the Front Lounge, the Globe, Hogan's, the Parliament and Zanzibar. Similarly, the atmosphere in many other well-known landmark pubs changes after a certain time of the evening. The staff clear away tables and chairs for greater circulation space and crank up the sound system to get older people out and a younger clientele in.

Some pubs have suffered from this insane commercialisation. Flannery's, the famous darts pub in Temple Bar, became a drinking hole of the same name and has been immortalised in every TV travel report since. The Foggy Dew in Fownes Street was a small pub frequented by many regulars of the Well Fed Café. The socialist, the gay rights activist and the twenty-something anarchist rubbed shoulders here for many years before the pub was renovated and frequented by the 'suits' from the local banks.

Nonetheless, the trade still survives. Although pubs now attract a very specific segment of the market for alcohol, the ordinary 'Dub' still identifies with a certain local pub. In the past, this allegiance reflected who he was. The loyal local was accepted as a member of a special club. Pubs were places where customers were equal to their neighbours − be they poets, merchants, soldiers or squires. The playing field was level. Regulars participated rather than acted as mere spectators: they talked, told a good story or sang a rousing song. The pub was like a stage with a cast of colourful characters, each with an improvised script. As an institution, it has helped a great oral tradition to survive.

WHAT WE DRINK NOW

IN 2004, the Drinks Industry Group of Ireland reported that alcohol sales were worth €6.4 billion to the economy. The breakdown of this figure reveals how drinking habits are changing. Wine consumption has grown by 14% and now accounts for 19% of the total market. Beer still dominates, with a share of about 53%. The consumption of spirits accounts for 18%. Although Irish people still go to the pub, more people are buying alcohol at off-licences and drinking at home. This is a far cry from how things were a century ago, when stout and ale were consumed by over 90% of the drinkers in pubs, and when claret and brandy were the favourite tipples in the gentlemen's clubs.

About 10% of the pubs in the country are in Dublin and over 30% of alcohol is consumed there. With the warming of the climate in Northern Europe, parts of southern England are now producing fine sparkling wines. Will we see a similar trend in the hills of Wicklow and West Cork? Could we buy a bottle of wine with a label claiming 'Wine of South Wicklow'?

LITERARY & HISTORIC PUBS
(and a Café)

THE DUKE

9 DUKE STREET, DUBLIN 2

THERE HAVE always been pub crawls in Dublin. As far back as the seventeenth century, Trinity students earned a reputation for rampaging through the city's taverns, no doubt declaiming from the works of Virgil, Ovid and Homer. The rhetorical powers of Cicero surely featured among college law students on their own bar hop. Before and after the Second World War, writers, like in any other trade, networked from pub to pub, making connections with newspapermen to get their work into print.

The Duke is the first stop on the trail of the *Dublin Literary Pub Crawl*. The tour originated in the Abbey Mooney on Abbey Street in 1988 but the pub closed down in 1989. The tour moved to its new home at the Bailey on Duke Street but it closed its doors five years later.

Duke Street lies just off Grafton Street and is part of the most prosperous neigbourhood in the city. Land values are at their highest in this quarter of a square mile. The architecture in this district is Georgian, although it is not as splendid as those residences around the corner, on Fitzwilliam Square and Merrion Square. The Duke pub carries on its trade in a building dating back to the eighteenth century and it has the second oldest licence in the area. With a hotel nearby and the terminus of the Bianconi stagecoach dropping off travellers from all parts of the country, this area must have been teeming with life in days gone by.

The street was famous for fresh oysters, which were served daily in many hostelries. In 1900, The Dive Oyster Restaurant was at 8 Duke Street. In this century, the only pub on the street to serve oysters is Davy Byrne's.

In 1904 Mrs. Kiernan from Longford took over The Dive and so began the connection with this Shannon-side county, from where the present owner hails. Mrs Kiernan was the mother of Catherine 'Kitty' Kiernan, who became engaged to Michael Collins, the leader of the Irish War of Independence. He had many 'safe houses' around the city and the site of the Duke was one of them.

In the 1970s, Larry Tobin owned a tiny pub here and hosted some of the liveliest writers and musicians south of the river. Paul Hewson (Bono of U2) was a regular in the decade before he and fellow band members achieved international recognition.

Duke Street is named after the second Duke of Grafton and Viceroy of Ireland in the seventeenth century. Grafton Street, South Anne Street and Harry Street were all developed by Joshua Dawson, who gave his name to the avenue that runs alongside the east of Duke Street. In keeping with developer tradition he built a beautiful house for himself on the street (now the Mansion House). Watch out for the plaque on the corner of Duke Street and Dawson Street, where Leopold Bloom stops and thoughtfully asks a blind man if he wants to cross the road.

THE BAILEY

2 DUKE STREET, DUBLIN 2

THIS ONCE-GREAT political and literary pub is now a shadow of its former self. The minimalist décor panders to a certain audience of urbanites but there is a wealth of history here that should be remembered when you sit on the terrace nursing a beer.

In 1680, the area around Duke Street was a marshy piece of land without even a lane crossing it. That all changed in 1705, when Joshua Dawson developed the area for residential use. By the 1850s, the Bailey was advertising its culinary delights of hot joints of beef and oyster sauce for a shilling. The kitchen even did a take-out service and delivered free of charge to all parts of the city. In 1837, John Bailey bought 2 Duke Street and began to advertise it as a 'shellfish tavern'. Oliver St John Gogarty recalled that the Bailey was a house of the muses, a 'place with the best whiskey and the best beef steak in Dublin'.

Writers and politicians flocked to the Bailey throughout the twentieth century. The most influential figure was Charles Stuart Parnell. He was the leader of the Irish Party in the House of Commons and fondly called the 'uncrowned king of Ireland'. You will notice his statue at the north end of O'Connell Street, pointing symbolically towards a national parliament for the Irish people. A room was reserved for him upstairs at the Bailey. It was called the Parnell Smoking Room. The MP from Avondale used the room regularly to discuss strategy and survival with his supporters before wandering around to his rooms at the hotel at the bottom of Dawson Street. James Joyce, himself a regular in the bars on Duke Street, remembers Parnell in his first poem (written at the age of nine) where he compares him to

> An eagle in his quaint perched aerie on the crags of time,
> Where the rude din of a new century
> Can trouble him no more

The National Library

© Failte Ireland

They were eloquent words from a nine year old boy. Joyce's father was delighted with his son's first offering and promised to send the poem off to the Vatican.

The poets Pádraig Colum and Thomas Kettle both visited the Bailey when William Hogan was the owner. Kettle was a lieutenant in the Royal Dublin Fusiliers and was killed in Guinchy during the Great War. He once wrote that Ireland 'could only become truly Irish if she first became European'.

Arthur Griffith, founder of Sinn Féin, often spent the evening in the Bailey after a day of reading at the National Library on Kildare Street. During the Anglo-Irish Treaty negotiations in London, which he attended, Winston Churchill observed that Griffith was 'an unusual figure, a silent Irishman'.

After Hogan's death in 1945, the reputation of the Bailey suffered but it still attracted visitors like Peter Ustinov, Evelyn Waugh, John

Betjeman, Margot Fonteyn and even Charles Chaplin. They were all anxious to taste the food and inhale the atmosphere of this famous tavern.

In 1957, John Ryan took over the pub and a second Golden Age began. The poet, painter and publisher–turned–publican hosted many famous evenings of the new literati of Dublin in the 1950s. J.P. Donleavy and Brendan Behan frequented the pub. Behan read an early draft of *The Ginger Man* and made notes in the margins, some of which Donleavy incorporated into the final text, which first appeared in 1955. The book had to be published in Paris by Maurice Girodias, widely disrespected as a publisher of dirty books (including *Lolita* by Vladimir Nabokov). For Donleavy it was to be a turning point away from repetitive poverty.

When the play of Donleavy's novel came to the stage in 1958, it got one airing in Dublin's Gaiety Theatre. The power of the Catholic Hierarchy was absolute at that time and the show was pulled because of clerical pressure. Sean O'Faolain remarked: 'The light word from this quarter (the Hierarchy) is tantamount to the raising of a sword'. A wake took place in the Bailey. Richard Harris played the central character and announced that he would seek an audience with Archbishop John Charles McQuaid. He said that if he got no satisfaction, a copy of the script should be dispatched to the Pope in Rome. Despite all the bravado, *The Ginger Man* would not be staged again in Dublin for almost thirty years.

The Bailey was part of the Brown Thomas department store building, which was bought by Marks and Spencer in 1994. The pub and landmark restaurant were closed and quickly gutted, prompting a controversy about where to put the door of 7 Eccles Street, the fictional home of Leopold Bloom (the door had been part of the foyer of the Bailey). Thankfully, the door found a new home at the James Joyce Centre on North Great Georges Street, where it enhances the excellent permanent exhibition that transferred there from the National Library.

DAVY BYRNE'S

21 DUKE STREET, DUBLIN 2

PERHAPS 'WORLD famous' is a bloated description for this
'moral pub' (as it was referred to in *Ulysses*) but it does have a wealth
of historical connections and literary lore. There was a real Davy
Byrne. He hailed from County Wicklow and bought the pub for just
over £2,000 in 1889. The Bailey pub across the street was owned
by a Mr Joyce and the writer, perhaps to avoid confusion, chose not
to favour it in his novel *Ulysses*. Instead, he preferred Davy Byrne's
as the setting for the *Lestrogonians* episode of the novel. The literary
connection has paid off handsomely.

Leopold Bloom, the everyman Jew in *Ulysses*, walked into the pub
after recoiling from the Burton restaurant (and billiard room) at
18 Duke Street, where he had seen the lunchtime eaters 'slopping
in their stews and pints'. Bloom orders the Gorgonzola cheese
sandwich and a glass of burgundy. Nosey Flynn badgers the owner
for a tip for the Ascot Gold Cup. Bloom observes the uncontrollable
movements of Flynn's nose to great comic effect. He also notices the
nice quiet atmosphere of the pub, the quality of the wooden counter
and how it 'curves just there'. In Bloom's day, the shelves behind the
bar were filled with sardine tins and Plumtree's Potted Meat.

Joyce's best-known novel was published by Sylvia Beach, a Paris
bookshop owner. When she met Joyce at a literary gathering she
remembered how 'he put his limp boneless hand into my tough
little paw'. She had met her literary god. The publication of *Ulysses*
in 1922 led to a pilgrimage to this pub. It began as a trickle but
turned into a flood after the first Bloomsday celebration in 1954.
The idea came about after pub conversations between John Ryan,
Tony Cronin and Brian O'Nolan. A group of literary enthusiasts
and Joyceans would follow in the footsteps of the characters from
Joyce's novel, re-enacting some of the episodes and reading from the
book. Bloomsday has become an annual event for Joyce aficionados
and *poseurs* alike. Davy Byrne's transforms itself into an Edwardian
fashion show, where Dubliners and literary tourists don boaters

and declaim from the novel. It is lots of fun, although one world-famous poet gets out of the city on 16 June to avoid the pretentious commotion.

Davy Byrne's has been blessed by its proximity to The Dáil, the Mansion House and the Catholic University on St Stephen's Green. Joyce and fair-weather student friends like Oliver St John Gogarty frequented the pub. James Stephen, whom Joyce chose to finish Finnegan's Wake, also favoured 'DBs'. Others were here too. Beckett was remembered as a remote figure in the pub in the 1930s. He hated the 'indiscretion and broken glass' of the Dublin pub scene. A galaxy of mid-century writers also inhabited 'Davy's': Patrick Kavanagh, Myles Na gCopaleen and Brendan Behan.

Street plaque of *Ulysses*

The founding fathers of the Irish Free State met upstairs. Members of the outlawed cabinet of the Provisional Government including Michael Collins (the 'soldier, not statesman') and Arthur Griffith (first President of the new state) both imbibed in the pub during the turbulent years of 1919 to 1922, when the Irish Free State came into being. There is a well-worn story of the barman calling time in the pub only to be told by a regular, 'Time be damned! Aren't half the cabinet sitting upstairs'. A free bottle of wine was offered to Griffith when the Treaty was signed to bring in self-government after 800 years.

In 1942, the Doran family took over and introduced an exotic touch. Barmen in white coats and black dicky bows served cocktails like a Manhattan, a Tom Collins or an Arsenic and Old Lace to the new cosmopolitan crowd. The novelist Edna O'Brien allows two characters from *The Girl With the Green Eyes* to order one Pernod between them. They drowned it with water so it would last them the night. The kindly barman took pity on them and augmented their drink with two glasses of beer. The new era of serving cocktails was an Americanisation too far for some regulars, including Flann O'Brien.

Cecil Salkeld (Brendan Behan's father-in-law) was commissioned to paint the murals on the right-hand wall of the main bar. He used well-known faces of Dublin in the 1940s, including Davy Byrne. Five beautiful statues (sculpted by Eddie Delaney and John Behan) stand behind the bar and contemplate the customers looking at them. The figures represent all the branches of the creative arts: literature, music, painting, drama and science.

The art deco styling is still here and the whole atmosphere is mischievously observed by Bernard Shaw, Flann O'Brien and the Shakespearian actor Michael MacLiammoir, who look down on us from Salkeld's beautiful murals, Morning, Noon and Evening. Of course, Leopold Bloom is a member of the ensemble that is watching the ebb and flow of this pub's trade.

McDAID'S

3 HARRY STREET, DUBLIN 2

A dour little pub — John Ryan

JUST AROUND the corner in Harry Street (off Grafton Street), you will find two venerable pubs: McDaid's and Bruxelles. The street was named after Harry Dawson, a member of the family who developed many of the streets in the area. McDaid's stands on the site of the old city morgue. The pub even fronted as a church for a time. One can verify this by climbing the rickety stairs to the first floor and looking above the bar at the old balcony, where the congregation boisterously sang hymns.

McDaid's was the headquarters of the post-war generation of writers that frequented the pubs and cafés around Grafton Street. They were described as a 'literary circle' – more like a half a dozen writers in the same town who 'cordially' hated each other. Drink entered them all like the 'Holy Spirit'.

A cast of very colourful characters have graced its dusty corners. Free artistic expression was the rule in this pub. Censorship or political correctness had no control over the conversation. The talk covered a diverse range of subjects – artistic, political and sporting – that would not have been tolerated in the more strait-laced pub run by an ever-pious publican. If you could hold your end up in this rarefied atmosphere, you were welcome. To be admitted to the round of drink-buying was a mark of intellectual respect. Money was scarce after the war and a writer earned no more than £5 for a published story. Such a fee went a long way in a pub and there were plenty in the round to help spend it.

The bawdy Brendan Behan turned up in McDaid's after his incarceration in prison in 1939. He had taken part in a failed bombing campaign at the Liverpool docks and was sent down for three years. In 1942, he arrived home to Ireland as a political hero and he drank out on it as often as he could. He entertained everyone, bursting into song and telling the most ribald stories from his limitless cache. Dublin was the perfect place for him to play out his role as an actor/raconteur but the city did not help him to get any work done. Behan came under the constant scrutiny of the Special Branch of the Garda Siochána (Irish police) but more often landed in gaol for being drunk and disorderly. After one such episode he was court-martialled by the IRA for 'bringing the movement into disrepute'. He was sentenced to death and told to show up for his execution. According to pub legend, Behan replied, 'You tried me in my absence. You can shoot me in my absence'.

McDaid's came to be dominated by Patrick Kavanagh. An enormous gauche man, he was known as the 'peasant poet' from County Monaghan. His writing day began soon after dawn. Then the pubs and the racetracks opened. A visit to Parson's bookshop on Baggot Street Bridge would follow, a scoop or two in the Waterloo or Searson's across the street, and then a short walk to Dawson Street. He would have passed 63 Baggot Street, where the artist Francis Bacon was born. Bacon's London studio has been reconstructed in the wonderful Dublin City Gallery on Parnell Square.

Kavanagh would end up at the bar in McDaid's, studying the racing form. The area around Grafton Street was favoured with several betting shops (*See* BOOKMAKERS PAGE 35) to assist the serious punter. Kavanagh conversed on all manner of subjects: from professional boxing to the beauty of Ginger Rogers, or the dire state of Gaelic football in Ulster. The barman who listened to him was the legendary Paddy O'Brien. He stage-managed a fine cast of characters. He was a firm diplomat – he had to be, considering the line-up of customers that entered this pub.

Another poet to 'provoke the regulars' in McDaid's was Belfast man Louis MacNeice. Michael Longley – then a student at Trinity – ran shy of introducing himself to his fellow Northerner shortly before MacNeice died in 1963. Longley tried instead to coax Kavanagh to be interviewed for the college magazine, but to no avail. Longley recalls that Kavanagh preferred to buy him 'pints and chasers over several rollicking hours' in the pub.

McDaid's began to rock just after the war when students from the exotic United States arrived to study here (under the GI Bill). Gainor Christ, who became the inspiration for Sebastian Dangerfield in J. P. Donleavy's *The Ginger Man*, was an habitué. According to barman Jim Gallagher, Christ was 'a nice quiet person…a kind and gentle soul' – quite a contrast to the vulgar ne'er-do-well depicted in the novel.

An eclectic mix of foreigners made McDaid's their home. They included the Nobel prize-winning German physicist Erwin Schrödinger, who escaped Nazi Germany during the war. He worked

in Dublin's Institute for Advanced Studies until he retired in 1955. On many an evening in McDaid's he warmed to his pet subject — wave mechanics — with anyone who cared to listen.

In 1895, Owen Farrelly — a grocer, and tea and wine merchant — ran his business here. In 1936, John McDaid (a Donegal man) paid £14,000 to put his name over the door. In 1970, Paddy O'Brien tried to buy the pub. No Dublin publican was going to bid against him but interest was keen from abroad, as this was such a famous literary pub. The premises fell to the auction hammer at £87,000, but O'Brien could not match that price. He took himself off to Grogan's on Castle Street. Having served many of the great pub writers — some of whom were now dead — O'Brien drew most of McDaid's clientele to the venue opposite the beautiful Powerscourt House. The new owners never did get their literary pub.

Nowadays, to get to McDaid's, you pass the endearing statue of Dublin rocker Phil Lynott, who 'came back to town' in August 2006. Lynott joins Elvis Presley, Freddie Mercury and Jimi Hendrix: that elite group of rock musicians who have been honoured with a statue in their home town. Across from McDaid's is Bruxelles (formerly known as Mooney's), which is decorated with signed portraits of many of the rising stars who gigged there. It is attractively finished in the Flemish gothic style, with a staircase turret overhanging the street.

Next door to McDaid's is Berry Bros & Rudd (wine merchants). The building, which dates from the 1880s, served as the city's Weights and Measures Office. Many of the tools of that trade are on display in the shop. Everything from the weight of a bag of coal to the grading of eggs was regulated from this building.

Dubliners may have turned towards the consumption of wine, but visitors will not often be served a premium glass of 'the grape' in a pub. Wine is bought for consumption at home, while beer, stout, ale and all manner of alcopops are drunk in the local pub. There are few dedicated wine bars in the city. It is one custom that should be introduced from London.

OPENING HOURS

PUBS NOW open from 10.30am to 11.30pm on Monday to Thursday but they stay open until 12.30am on Friday and Saturday. Pubs close at 11pm on Sundays. These closing times refer to 'last orders' – customers still have another thirty minutes to drink up. However, this is not set in stone. It depends on the publican and how relaxed he or she is about enforcing the law. This quaint Irish custom differs radically from the experience in the United Kingdom, where the landlord is physically pulling the glass out of your hand ten minutes after closing time.

NEARY'S

1 CHATHAM STREET, DUBLIN 2

THE VISITOR will always be drawn to Neary's pub by the beautiful cast-iron arms holding up two lanterns outside the main entrance.

This late-Victorian pub is a great place to meet people for a quiet drink. The rear of the pub backs onto the stage door of the Victorian Gaiety Theatre, and so Neary's is often thick on the ground with thespians and prominent figures from the entertainment business. Place them beside the weary Grafton Street shopper and you will get a feel for the type of clientele that frequent this beautiful pub.

In the 1860s, the pub was known as Casserley's Tavern. When Leo Neary took over, he attracted many supporters of racing and hunting. Across the laneway, the Gaiety Theatre has played host to many fine opera companies from around the world, and Dubliners still go there for the annual Christmas Panto. It was here that the actor Alan Devlin stunned his audience during a performance of *H.M.S. Pinafore*. During the first act, he exclaimed 'Oh f**k it! I can't do it. I'm going home'. Legend has it that the stage manager was tearing off his Admiral's costume in Tangier Lane outside Neary's to put it on a petrified understudy. The opening scene of the award-winning movie *Once* is set at the entrance to the lane, on the corner of Grafton Street.

Neary's was one of the many spiritual homes of Flann O'Brien, when he was not in McDaid's (Harry Street) or the Bailey (Duke Street). He would meet the popular musical comedy star Jimmy O'Dea, who popped in through the back door during an interval at the Gaiety Theatre. John Ryan, publisher of the magazine *Envoy*, brought the partially blind English poet John Heath-Stubbs into Neary's. His book *Remembering How We Stood* tells how they repaired to a nearby bookmakers (on South Anne Street) after several drinks. Heath-Stubbs had never been to a betting office and, hearing the noise of booze-smelling customers, he leaned on the nearest counter and called for another round of drinks for his friends.

Chatham Street was named after the son of the first Earl of Chatham. Balfe Street, just around the corner, had been known as Pitt Street, which was named after English Prime Minister William Pitt.

THE GAIETY THEATRE

JUST BEHIND Neary's is the Gaiety Theatre on South King Street. It reopened in 2003, after extensive refurbishment. It is now a 1,200-seater venue but could accomodate 2,000 punters when it first opened 170 years ago. John Gunn founded the theatre in 1871 and a bust honours him on the main staircase. The 'old lady' on South King Street retains much of its gay Victorian magic, with plush velvet seating replacing the rickety worn-out chairs from an earlier fit. The latest restoration soaked up €2.2 million of the owners' money but Denis and Caroline Desmond also benefited from state aid to the tune of €7.8 million.

Outside on the newly pedestrianized street, stars from the world of theatre have been invited to leave their hand prints on the

pavement to mark their contribution to Irish entertainment. The best known of them are the grand dame of musical comedy Maureen Potter and the renowned Italian tenor Luciano Pavarotti.

The Gaiety was not just known as a variety hall. Opera, ballet and the serious play have featured on the programme. Indeed, the first production to play here in 1871 was Oliver Goldsmith's *She Stoops To Conquer*. One of the ground-breaking plays of the twentieth century opened in the theatre in September 1964. *Philadelphia Here I Come*, set in Donegal, had a traditional backdrop of a shop and a back kitchen but the play was revolutionary in its portrayal of the central character's inner and outer selves. The play's theme of emigration resonated with audiences everywhere. *Philadelphia* also launched the playwright Brian Friel onto the world stage.

CAFÉ EN SEINE

39 DAWSON STREET, DUBLIN 2

THIS IS a giant of a pub – the T-Rex of the trade. A book about Dublin pubs would not be complete without this *fin de siècle* piece of kitsch. From the subdued lighting to the expansive mirrors (each costing around €2,000) and the Grecian urns adorned with nubile girls, this pub plays host to the executive class of Dublin. It is a trendy pub and, like so many of them, it is big, brash and 'out there'. The über-fashionable come here. Café En Seine serves the floating urban population (in their twenties, thirties and forties) who socialise after work.

English footballers and their WAGs have come here to be wowed by the decadence and over-the-top décor, and perhaps to spot the glamorous models who frequent the pub. Tall plants reach up to the vaulted ceiling searching for light. There are three bars, and hot food and sandwiches are available throughout the day.

It adds up to everything a traditional Dublin pub should not be – but it works. The food is good too, comfortable seating is *de rigueur*, and the Sunday afternoon jazz is tuneful. As in many pubs, there are two atmospheres at work. On weekend nights, the upwardly mobile men and women of the 'new Ireland' can be seen schmoozing here. In the daytime, the mood is laid back. Although the lighting gives the effect of a bordello, locals and tourists can be seen wiling away the hours, contemplating the authenticity of the stylish fixtures and fittings.

DOHENY & NESBITT

4–5 LOWER BAGGOT STREET, DUBLIN 2

THIS PUB is a favourite of journalists, civil servants and those with key influence in Irish life. D&Ns was completely refurbished when the present owner employed architect James O'Connor to enlarge the tiny pub with a seamless wood-panelled room at the back. This

© Failte Ireland

new area, complete with snug and partitions, appears as old as the original chamber at the front and is a great example of how an old Dublin pub can be revitalised.

The pub was known as Delahunty's tea and wine merchant on Bloomsday 1904. Before that, from the last years of the Great Famine, William Burke held the license to sell beer, wine and most other merchandise, as was the custom in those days. The pub benefits from a large influx of members of the chattering classes who work close by in the many offices of Georgian Dublin. The *Sunday Tribune* newspaper is published a couple of doors away. In 1980, this tabloid Sunday paper was founded by John Mulcahy, with Conor Brady as its first editor. Naturally, the information stream (gossip) about government goings-on flows here to the staff of the 'Turbine'.

Ned Doheny and Tom Nesbitt gained considerable experience in the US and saw the virtue of retaining the old marble-topped tables, pump handles, and dark corners that are ideal for the quiet *tête-à-tête*. The pub is a well-known hunting ground for ladies of a certain vintage in pursuit of the elusive but ageing Irish bachelor.

Many an inmate of this revered pub can also be seen in that other Dublin institution, the Horse Shoe Bar at the Shelbourne Hotel. When you walk the short distance between both venues you will pass the Huguenot Graveyard, which is dedicated to the 239 families buried there. They were among those French Protestants who migrated to Ireland in the seventeenth century to escape persecution during the Counter Reformation.

IRISH COFFEE

Only Irish coffee provides in a single glass all four essential food groups – alcohol, caffeine, sugar and fat.

Alex Levine

ON A miserable night in 1942, the passengers who got off a transatlantic flight at Foynes Airfield in County Limerick were served coffee by the head chef, Joseph Sheridan. Looking at the physical condition of his subjects, Sheridan decided to put a shot of whiskey into the mix to warm them up.

The exhausted travellers were so impressed that one of them asked, 'Buddy, is this Brazilian coffee?' Sheridan replied, 'No, it's Irish coffee'. Nowadays, there are variations on the theme. Bailey's Irish Coffee substitutes the essential ingredient and Kentucky Coffee does likewise with a shot of Bourbon.

HOW TO MAKE IT PROPERLY. There are four ingredients to a good Irish Coffee: cream, coffee, sugar and whiskey. Heat a whiskey goblet. Add in a good measure of Irish whiskey and a spoon of sugar. Then add strong black coffee and stir well. Pour lightly whipped cream over the back of a spoon to slow down its arrival on top of the coffee. The sugar will keep the cream floating at the top, preserving the definition between black and white.

Finally, sip and savour, and wait for the concoction to take effect.

TONERS

139 LOWER BAGGOT STREET, DUBLIN 2

THE DARK wood and ornate partitions of this fine pub tell the story of a tavern that has changed little since it was opened by Andrew Rogers in 1842. He moved from 94 Baggot Street to set up here as a grocer and wine merchant. In 1886, the grant of arms from Dublin Castle hung over the door to proclaim a new owner, John O'Neill, as grocer to the Lord Lieutenant.

James Toner was trading here in 1923, during the Civil War. According to literary legend, W. B. Yeats was placed in the quiet of the snug one day soon after he returned from Oxford in 1922. Oliver St John Gogarty was responsible for setting the milestone in motion when he offered Yeats a sherry from the bar. The poet quaffed the liquid, rose to his considerable height, and said, 'I have seen a pub. Will you kindly take me home'. The story may be an embellishment, as Yeats was known to drink in the Old Cheshire Cheese pub, off Fleet Street in London. The Rhymer's Club, which he co-founded with Ernst Rhys in 1890, met there until 1904.

Back in Dublin, Gogarty and George Moore both had rooms just around the corner, on Ely Place. Bram Stoker's brother Thornley also lived on the street. It was developed by Sir Gustavus Hume, a surgeon and property speculator who leased the first house to the Earl of Ely. Some buildings were destroyed to make way for the excellent Gallagher Gallery, which houses artworks from the Royal Hibernian Academy.

Property speculation featured in the part destruction of the once beautiful Hume Street, which runs into Ely Place. In the 1970s, a keenly fought battle for its conservation merely ensured that Georgian houses on the corner of St Stephen's Green were torn down and reproduced in the same style. If you stand opposite Hume Street, you can compare the real with the 'retro'.

KEHOE'S

9 SOUTH ANNE STREET, DUBLIN 2

THIS TRADITIONAL Dublin pub is located on South Anne Street (often confused with Duke Street). The street, which was

© Failte Ireland

laid out by Joshua Dawson, offers wonderful views of St Anne's Church when the fitful Dublin sun chooses to shine. Kehoe's was one of Dublin's busiest boozers before the advent of the superpub a decade ago. It is adorned with nicely carved partitions that lend an air of intimacy to the place. A narrow bar at the front and a bigger lounge at the back complete the accommodation downstairs.

When John Kehoe (the owner) died a few years ago, the bar was sold for over 2 million Irish *punts* to well-known publican Louis Fitzgerald. To his credit, he changed almost nothing about the place, except to open the musty interior upstairs, where Mr Kehoe had lived. The new owners set up a bar in the old living quarters, creating a parlour atmosphere with comfortable seating.

Kehoe's is just across the road from what was the Adelphi Hotel (20–21 South Anne Street). Joyce mentioned it in *A Portrait of the Artist as a Young Man*. The pub was owned and run by Dan McGowan on Bloomsday in 1904. Kehoe's was one of many pubs along the street and complemented the businesses of Grafton Street, which was

© Failte Ireland

dominated by silk mercers, linen drapers and shirt makers. A century ago, the variety of shops on Dublin's premier street stretched to antique dealers, carpet warehouses, fruit and flower shops and a good selection of cafés and restaurants. That choice has been dramatically eroded by the dominance of British chain stores that can afford the exorbitant rents on this high street. In Joyce's time, the street sounded to 'hoofthuds low-ringing' because Grafton Street was then paved with hexagonal-shaped wooden blocks.

Watch out for the beautiful snug in Kehoe's, with its own separate entrance and serving hatch. The wooden drawers behind the bar are exactly as they were when customers came to purchase their favourite blend of tea or coffee. Spare a thought for the diverse mix

Inside Kehoe's Pub

of customers a century ago – those who shopped at the military boot makers at number 25 or bought a walking stick from the umbrella manufacturer ten doors away.

In 1812, Percy Bysshe Shelley stayed at 17 Grafton Street, around the corner from Kehoe's. He wandered down the avenue, to a bakery to buy bread for immediate consumption. He was deeply shocked by the poverty and destitution that he witnessed in Ireland. Even before he arrived, he had enough political savvy to write an *Address to the Irish People*. In the pamphlet, he argued for 'political and religious freedom' and sought to 'awake in the minds of the Irish poor a knowledge of their real state'. Well said, Mr Shelley!

THE SPIRIT GROCER

THE SPIRIT Grocers Act of 1791 was considered to be one of the most damaging licences to be granted in the city. A certificate of good character was not necessary to obtain this licence. Its effect was to lure many more people, particularly women, to alcoholism. They would become addicted behind the 'biscuit tins'.

The idea began innocently enough. If women were allowed to go into these shops to buy the daily groceries, they would not need to go to pubs. The social stigma attached to going into the public bar did not exist in the context of the spirit grocer. Partitions were deliberately constructed to divide the grocery counter from the section selling alcohol. Up to two quarts of liquor could be purchased here and consumed off the premises. Eventually, these shops became pubs. The authorities were reluctant to grant new pub licences but they freely granted licences to the grocers to sell alcohol. By the 1870s, nearly half of the 600 licences granted to spirit grocers in Ireland were in Dublin.

Many pubs continued to sell a variety of tea and coffee in the grocery section, but their partitions had to be adequate enough to distinguish the liquor section from the general shop selling household goods. The pub-cum-shop lasted until supermarkets put local grocers out of business. Coincidentally, it was about this time (in the 1960s) that the lounge bar appeared as the grocery counter disappeared from pubs.

BEWLEY'S
GRAFTON STREET, DUBLIN 2

The heart and hearth of Dublin. Brendan Kennelly

THE AROMA of roasting coffee along Grafton Street is the first sign that you are nearing Dublin's legendary 'clattery café'. It has been home to every type of citizen from the city's gene pool: shoppers, politicians, tourists, ne'er-do-wells, students and actors, and other praisers of their own past. The atmosphere is traditional, a reminder of the way Dublin was in grander times. The café patron can wile away an hour here in style, sitting in the plush booths on the high-ceilinged ground floor.

The consumption of tea grew dramatically after the Great Famine, and the Bewley family prospered as a result. They were one of 130 Quaker families who lived in the city. These families were generally well off and maintained close business connections. The 'cupán tae' habit took hold in the towns and cities but was less prevalent in the countryside. The Temperance movement helped to spread the idea that the consumption of hard liquor was at the root of many problems in Ireland. The expression 'tee-total' came into the English language in the 1830s. Taxes were reduced on tea and it no longer had to be kept under lock and key. Charles Bewley opened a store at 11 South Great George's Street, reflecting the strength of the market for tea consumption. It was not just for the genteel classes and those ladies of London who went on tea-drinking outings. Tea became part of the staple diet of the whole country by the turn of the twentieth century.

© Failte Ireland

From the 1890s onwards, Ernest Bewley ran the business and introduced the Oriental Cafés. He began by importing large consignments of coffee into Ireland. Coffee houses had been a feature of Dublin life since the seventeenth century when businessmen came together with writers and men of the professions. Ernest Bewley added extra flavour by giving demonstrations on coffee making and serving his wife's scones and buns. The idea was a hit.

The Bewley name first appeared on Grafton Street in 1927. Ireland was settling down to a period of peace and Ernest Bewley sited the new venture at the old Whytes Academy, whose past pupils included Richard Sheridan, W.B. Yeats, the Duke of Wellington and Robert Emmet. When you go there – and everybody does – admire Harry Clarke's famous stained glass windows while drinking your tea on a damp morning. Many Irish writers, including Elisabeth Bowen, Mary Lavin, James Plunkett and Thomas Kinsella, have enjoyed the tea and cakes in this great Dublin institution.

GROGAN'S

15 SOUTH WILLIAM STREET, DUBLIN 2

GROGAN'S IS a local pub. There are not many left in the centre of town. It stands opposite the beautiful eighteenth-century Powerscourt House shopping precinct. There were hundreds of these 'granite boxes' dotted around the country until the IRA burned most of them down during and after the War of Independence. The clientele of Powerscourt House would not automatically gravitate towards Grogan's for a pint – but they should. The brass plate beside the Castle Market door proclaims: Jointly owned by Paddy Kennedy and Tom Smith since 1973. The sign is a badge of honour to the owners, who keep a traditional pub going in the middle of this newly discovered trendy enclave. Artists and writers are well represented in this bohemian throwback, which fills the role held by McDaid's (Harry Street) and the Palace Bar (Fleet Street) in the past. There is a real pub culture here. People talk and others listen. Some eavesdrop and others commune silently with their pint of stout.

Grogan's is democratic in the way that a pub should be. It also has cross-generational appeal. You can rub shoulders with anyone here.

© Failte Ireland

The pub has not compromised to the whims of fashionable pub fit-outs; if anything it is a tad shabby. Here you will see the grumpy and cantankerous 'Dub' – opining in his bittersweet way. However, if you have a 'well stocked mind' then you will get a fair hearing in this pub. You will not get away with bragging about your property portfolio in Grogan's. Absent from the old days are the cigarette smoke and the *Evening Press*. Still present is the toasted sandwich and packet soup for lunch. Nobody complains, though.

Grogan's, like the solid Dublin citizen, has its principles. Chief among them is not to entertain change for the sake of it. That is why is has such a loyal following, among young and old alike, certain that they will bump into a familiar face, even if it is just the owner's.

Dakota — close by at 6 South William Street — represents the polar opposite in pub styles. The contrast is worth observing. Originally a fabric warehouse for a department store, the pub is long — over 50 metres long. The décor now is sleek, sexy and knowing. There is art on the walls but no signatures to tell us who painted them. This pub could be anywhere in the world. The feeling is international and the servers are a cosmopolitan mix of nationalities. 'What's wrong with that?' you might say. Nothing really, except the anonymity of the whole project. It is making a statement: comfortable and chic, with food during the day and face control on the door at night. The young in each other's arms come here. They seem to love it.

FALLON'S

129 THE COOMBE, DUBLIN 8

FALLON'S IS a small pub on the Coombe. The street gets its name from the Irish 'cum' meaning 'hollow place'. For many years, it was outside the city walls and thus beyond the control of Anglo-Norman laws. Fugitives were 'at liberty' here, hence the name given to the area: the Liberties. Before the Reformation, the Liberties covered about six acres of city streets, adjoining the Coombe and Spitalfields.

Fallon's has been trading under that name for over forty years, and it survived the wrecking ball that swung here in the 1980s. It is very popular with the wily antique dealers of Francis Street. It benefited from the smoking ban that came into force in 2003; the non-smoker can now breathe in this tiny jewel of a pub. It is a place where you can toast a friend or simply relax and unwind.

Dan Donnelly held the licence here in the early nineteenth century. He was a champion boxer and *bon viveur*, but he died penniless in 1843. Tens of thousands of Dubliners followed the hearse and saw his boxing gloves resting on a silk cushion upon the coffin. When the Famine struck two years later, John Tinnelly began trading here. One of his most famous customers was the blind balladeer Michael 'Zozimus' Moran. Tall and gaunt, he had lost his sight at two weeks old but made a lifelong living wandering around the poor quarters of Dublin in a scalloped cape and corduroy trousers, reciting self-penned poems and songs. One ditty was in praise of the high-octane poteen, a spirit distilled from potatoes in remote parts of the country:

> O long life to the man who invented poteen –
> Sure the Pope ought to make him a martyr –
> If myself was this moment Victoria, the Queen,
> I'd drink nothing but whiskey and wather (sic)

French Huguenots had settled in this area of the Liberties. By the early 1800s, though, there was little trace of them, except the trades they left behind: tanning, weaving, milling and silk. Nor will you see the famous 'Dutch Billy' properties that they designed: terraced houses with gabled fronts.

By the beginning of the nineteenth century, there were 55 breweries and 25 distilleries in Dublin. At that time, it was a city of contrasts. On the one hand, it was opulent, planned and grand. On the other, it was a place of disease, poverty and filth worse than that seen in most English cities. In 1798, Reverend James Whitelaw wrote about the living conditions for those in the Liberties:

> The streets are generally narrow; the houses crowded together. This crowded population wherever it obtains is almost universally accompanied by a very serious evil — Into the back yard of each house, frequently not ten feet deep, is flung from the windows of each apartment, the ordure and filth of its numerous inhabitants.

The Huguenots were not the only nationality to haunt the Liberties. Little Italy was also represented there. These Italians, like many first immigrants to a new country, knew very little English. According to Eamon MacThomais's book *Me Jewel and Darlin' Dublin*, the famous fish and chip order 'one and one' came from these immigrants having to point to what they wanted and say 'I'll have wan of that' (fish) 'and wan of that' (chips).

By the early twentieth century, the Liberties had become one of the main slum areas of the city. A close examination of Thom's directory shows 20 of the 129 premises on the Coombe listed as 'tenements'. The worst of them were right outside the door of Fallon's — and along Cork Street and Kevin Street. In many of the houses, it was not unusual to have fifteen people living in one room. Social workers and volunteers from the St Vincent de Paul (a charitable organisation) were often afraid to climb the four floors, as the staircases and banisters were so rotten.

Along Francis Street (north of Fallon's) you will find many antique shops, where you can browse for a bargain. It is worthwhile stopping to marvel at the Iveagh Market. It was commissioned by Lord Iveagh of the Guinness family and opened in 1907. He gifted the building to the city the following year. Although it ceased to function as a market in 1996, it may soon be redeveloped as an upmarket specialist food and retail arcade. Just off Francis Street is the redbrick enclave of John Dillon Street, where the whiskey family of John Power built houses for its workers. The units may be small but these sturdy, two-bedroomed maisonettes are ideal for contemporary city living. The area is named after the Irish parliamentarian John Dillon, who stood by the executed leaders of 1916 in a speech to the British House of Commons:

> *I know they were wrong but they fought a clean fight and they fought with superb bravery and skill. I declare most solemnly, and I am not afraid to say it in the House of Commons, that I am proud of these men.*

THE TEMPERANCE MOVEMENT

IN FEBRUARY 1843, Father Theobold Mathew wrote to a friend in America: 'I have now, with the Divine Assistance, hoisted the banner of Temperance in almost every parish in Ireland'. He had started the movement for total abstinence in Cork City five years earlier. He trained at Maynooth College and joined the Capuchin Order, rising to Provincial in 1828; he held that position for the next twenty three years.

It was as the Apostle of Temperance that he really made his mark. He toured the country and preached the word of self-discipline with great success. Drunkenness was not just a problem in Dublin and other cities; it was widespread around the country and common in all classes.

When Thackeray met Father Mathew in Cork in 1842, he wrote: 'No man seems more eager than he for the practical improvement of this country. Leases and rents, farming improvements, reading societies, music societies – he was full of these, and of his schemes of temperance above all'.

Temperance groups held public rallies and parades, and introduced coffee houses as an alternative to pubs. By the time Father Mathew had held his third public meeting in Dublin, 173,000 had pledged allegiance to his doctrine of sobriety. The new mood prompted the closure of scores of breweries and distilleries, reducing both owners and workers to destitution. In less than six years (from 1838 to 1845), Father Mathew reduced the number of taverns around Ireland from 21,300 to just over 13,000.

There is a commemorative statue of Father Mathew on O'Connell Street.

THE LORD EDWARD

23 CHRISTCHURCH PLACE, DUBLIN 8

ONE OF the last pieces of the medieval wall of Dublin still stands on Lamb Alley, around the corner from John Dillon Street. Be sure to see it before you exit from this maze of little streets. Next you will see the imposing profile of Christ Church Cathedral. You are now in the heart of Medieval Dublin. Nearby (at 23 Christchurch Place, Dublin 8) is The Lord Edward pub – a beautiful Victorian tavern with a 'quare-shaped' marble counter and intimate snug in one corner. Seafood aficionados will find the city's oldest specialist restaurant upstairs. If the food here does not appeal, you can nip around the corner to the legendary Burdock's on Werburgh Street for take-away fish and chips. Leo Burdock started the business in 1913, and it has been a post-pub institution ever since. Line up with cabinet ministers, students and party animals and taste the difference.

Many houses in this area were listed as tenements in 1904 but they were cleared away during the Free State government's first term. They were replaced by bakers and bootmakers when Thomas Cunniam ran his pub on this site in 1930.

The pub takes its name from Edward Fitzgerald, aristocrat and revolutionary. He was a son of the first Duke of Leinster. He joined the United Irishmen in 1796 and became a leading advocate of an uprising three years later. He took no part in the fighting, though, as he was wounded while being arrested shortly before hostilities broke out. He died in Newgate prison on 4 June 1798. Yeats honoured Edward Fitzgerald in his poem September 1913

> Was it for this the wild geese spread
> The grey wing upon every tide;
> For this that all that blood was shed,
> For this Edward Fitzgerald died,
> And Robert Emmet and Wolfe Tone,
> All that delirium of the brave?

Fitzgerald is buried in St Werburgh's Church (which is just around the corner). This church has a fine interior, and the carved pulpit was designed by Francis Johnston. Curiously, the church has no spire. Popular wisdom held that the builders were prevented from erecting a tower high enough to overlook Dublin Castle. John Field, who wrote several Nocturnes, was baptised here in 1782.

ST PATRICK'S CATHEDRAL

SAINT PATRICK'S Cathedral is a place of worship and a museum to the Anglo-Irish dead. Nowadays, it sustains itself with the constant flow of visitors (around 300,000 a year) to the beautiful Gothic church, which is modelled on Salisbury Cathedral in England. A good place to begin exploring here is with the monstrous Boyle monument, erected for the famous physicist. St Patrick's Well and baptismal font, where the patron saint is supposed to have converted the first Christians of the city, can be found opposite the entrance. The font had been in a small church outside the city wall, on an islet of the Poddle (an underground tributary of the Liffey).

In the twelfth century, Archbishop Comyn was the first Anglo-Irish bishop to be seated here and he embarked on a building campaign that lasted from 1192 to 1270. He also started a fight for religious dominance over Christ Church, just up the road. He wanted to establish his own jurisdiction on the English model, while Christ Church was established under Augustinian rules adapted to Ireland and approved by St Malachy. This spiritual turf war lasted until the Reformation. In 1213, the church was raised to the status of cathedral by Comyn's successor, Henry of London, one of the signatories of the Magna Carta two years later.

The church is cruciform in shape. The current structure was renovated by the Guinness family and is almost 100 metres in length. The interior pillars show signs of water damage from several floods over the centuries. Two pieces of furniture are worthy of note. The first is the moveable pulpit that was used to carry Swift to remoter parts of the church to wake up dozy members of his congregation. The second is inside the altar rail – rows of seats for the Knights of Saint Patrick, with the ceremonial sword, crest and helmet above each chair. To make it into this exclusive club, each knight had to be a 'gentleman of blood without reproach and descended of three descents of noblesse'. The knights were similar to the members of the Knights of the Garter and the Scottish Order of the Thistle.

© Failte Ireland

Families and counties are remembered affectionately by coats-of-arms on the cushions that hang on the pews around the church. British military might is also remembered with flags positioned in repose to honour Irishmen who fought in the many campaigns across the British Empire.

A curious door – with a hole in the middle – can be found in the church. In the early sixteenth century, an ongoing feud between the rival Butler (Ormond) and Geraldine (Fitzgerald) clans came to a head in the churchyard of the cathedral. The Earl of Ormond eventually took refuge behind the door of the Chapter House. The two principals made their peace by cutting a hole in the door and shaking hands – or 'risking an arm'. The door now symbolises peace and reconciliation between 'Catholic, Protestant and Dissenter' in Ireland – and it launched a new saying into the English language.

Turlough O'Carolan – 'the last of the Irish bards' – is commemorated in the cathedral. He was just eighteen when he was blinded by smallpox. He was a friend of Jonathan Swift, and has been described as the last of the wandering poet-minstrels of Ireland. Swift, though, is the most famous internee here. His tomb is to the right of the main entrance.

Douglas Hyde – 'that fine and scholarly old gentleman' (according to FDR) – is honoured in a monument almost next to Swift. Hyde became the first President of Ireland in 1938 and was widely respected for his work in helping to save the Irish language from extinction. His movement, under the banner of the Gaelic League, was to gain a mass following throughout the island.

THE LONG HALL

51 SOUTH GREAT GEORGE'S STREET, DUBLIN 2

IN THE eighteenth century, coaches and other modes of transport set out from South Great George's Street to Rathmines and farther afield. The street was originally called George's Lane and then named after England's patron saint. However, you will not find the St George's flag flying in the street's best-known hostelry. The Long Hall was, if anything, a republican pub. The curate behind the bar was a 'member' and you could leave word with him and know that it was as safe as in a bank vault.

The style of the Long Hall allowed the owner to swiftly enter the pub and avoid troublesome customers or bill collectors lurking in the main bar. The pub that was built in the 1880s now resembles a long narrow corridor, occupied by regulars and visitors who gratefully stumble across it. Slattery's in Rathmines is another excellent example of the style.

There is a traditional square room at the back. Inevitably, the 'match on telly' takes over here but look around and you will see a magnificent set of prints — the *Town Criers of London* — depicting street sellers advertising their wares in English and French. Old copper bed-warmers hang decoratively from the walls. You will also note the guns decorating the walls, a reminder perhaps of one famous Fenian, 'Pagan' O'Leary, who frequented the pub in the 1860s.

POLITICAL PUBS

DURING THE War of Independence, pubs played a vital role as 'safe' houses for men and women in the movement. Many IRA pubs were on the northside of the city, where the population was predominantly working class and anti-British. Clandestine meetings were held in the snug or the back room. It helped that the barman knew each 'regular' by name and someone from outside was spotted immediately. Very often the publican and his curate were IRA members or sympathetic to the cause of freedom. Nevertheless, some publicans were frightened of any illegal activity taking place in their pubs, for fear that the licence would be revoked when it came up for renewal in front of a magistrate.

The existance of nooks, crannies and cellars in pubs made them ideal places to stash illegal weapons. Some pubs even had elaborate tunnels running underground to assist active members of the IRA to escape the long arm of English law. Political figures as important as Michael Collins and Dan Breen regularly used pubs to receive information and to plan the next guerrilla attack against the British Secret Service.

Dubliners always talked politics in the pub but such discussions made for a dangerous atmosphere. Blood was often spilt during arguments between opposing sides. Publicans tended to be wary of the subject because it invariably led to a row and a fistfight. After the bitterly fought Civil War in 1923, some publicans would not allow political discussion in their houses.

The Long Hall was a house painters' pub. The union office was just up the road. Brendan Behan would come here to get a day's work. It is worth viewing the bar from the back room; it exhibits itself beautifully, with dark stained gloss wood, gold leaf enhancements, bevelled glass and a counter dressed with copper trim. Convex distorting round mirrors are still to be seen behind the bar. The beautiful Mangan clock boasts the correct time for Dublin and completes the atmosphere in a pub where time seems to stand still (though not according to another clock in the pub, which reminds us that 'tempus fugit').

Outside, the street bustles with bars and restaurants. George's Street was originally developed after 1850, thanks to the business acumen of the Pim family. This Quaker clan ran one of Dublin's most famous department stores (at 73–88) until it was demolished in 1970. The poet Thomas Moore was born not far away – at 12 Aungier Street (dubbed 'danger street' by the locals). He is famous for his melodies, which influenced the singer John McCormack and tenor-turned-writer James Joyce. Visitors will pass Moore's statue at the junction of Westmorland

Street and College Green. The statue stands above a gentleman's public convenience. In *Ulysses*, Leopold Bloom delights in the pun: 'They did right to put him above a urinal. Meeting of the Waters'. The song of that name recalls a beauty spot in County Wicklow where the Avonmore and Avonbeg rivers converge. Keen TV viewers may be interested to know that the popular BBC series *Ballykissangel* was filmed in the neighbouring village of Avoca.

Further along this rapidly changing street, restaurants and new businesses are spliced in among new apartment buildings. Running south, George's Street becomes Aungier Street. Fronting onto it is the Roman Catholic Whitefriar Street Church run by the Carmelite Order. It was erected in 1825 by George Papworth who also built St Mary's Pro Cathedral. Romantics young and old will be heartened to know that Pope Gregory XVI donated the relics of St Valentine to the church in the nineteenth century (they had been kept at the Vatican).

The sound of seagulls reminds us that the river and docklands are never far away. If you walk northwards from the Long Hall towards the Liffey, you will see the magnificent turreted building of the George's Street market. This redbrick structure was the first custom-built shopping mall in the city, and it was opened in 1882. It replaced an older marketplace and slaughterhouse. Visitors could be forgiven for feeling that they were in London – Kensington High Street perhaps? That would not be surprising, as the architects were English and buildings of this style were often introduced to Ireland from original designs in the United Kingdom. Shops, stalls, clip joints and sandwich bars like the excellent Simon's Place and Honest to Goodness jostle together to make this market one of the liveliest enclaves off the tourist track. Simon's has a relaxed informality that is governed by the quiet authority of the owner. He watches over the 'gaff' with rubber-gloved hands plunged into a basin of dishes. The cheesecake is homemade, delicious and excellent value.

See if you can then find what amounts to a secret passage into the extravagant Market Bar, which is owned by gastro-publicans Eoin Foyle and Jay Burke. They have taken the unusual step of creating a 'talk only' pub in what was once an old warehouse. Now, you can graze on tapas all day and drink in a 'pipe down' atmosphere. No TV and no music is the policy here and guess what – customers love it!

Another bar to visit before you leave the George's Street strip is the excellent Havana Tapas Bar. Is it a restaurant or is it a bar? The owner prefers 'bar' but the choice of food prepared by chef Joey is flavoursome and substantial. The prices are keen too, especially for soup and hot sandwiches served on wooden platters at lunchtime. At night, the atmosphere turns South American as salsa music pulsates from all corners of the house. People dance here!

THE BRAZEN HEAD

20 BRIDGE STREET, DUBLIN 8

THIS PUB claims to be the oldest in Dublin. The gates of the Norman city were closed at night, and so many taverns sprang up around the city gate to house those travellers who did not get to the city on time – or those foreigners (that is, the Irish) who had to leave. The Brazen Head is one of two surviving pubs on this site. From here you can also see a reconstructed segment of the old city wall.

The bridge from which the street gets its name is now called after the Apostle of Temperance, Father Mathew. A bridge has crossed the Liffey here since the thirteenth century. The pub claims to have been built in 1198 but the building is a Georgian construction (around 1750). An archway once framed the entrance to this hotel and tavern but you now walk through a castellated gateway into the courtyard. The area came under the destructive eye of the road engineers but the pub was saved by a preservation order, as a nod to its age and the historical characters who came here. For many years, the writing table of the insurrectionist Robert Emmet could be seen in the pub. As the building stands within walking distance of the law courts, many of their 'eminences' from the legal profession have set off oratorical fireworks in the pub. The writer Flann O'Brien rubbed shoulders with the legal eagles in this oak tavern, having previously crossed swords with them in the debating chamber of University College Dublin.

The advocate Daniel O'Connell, the MP for County Clare and a pacifist all his life, met many of his clients here. He once said: 'The altar of liberty totters when it is cemented only with blood'. The higher echelons of the legal profession were barred to him because he was a Catholic. He eventually campaigned successfully for the granting of Catholic Emancipation in 1829. Another barrister and regular of the 'Brazen' was Tim Healy, who vehemently opposed Parnell after 'the blackbird of Avondale' was named as the third party in the famous divorce case involving Kitty O'Shea in 1890. Healy was rewarded with the position of Governor General of Ireland, which he held from 1922 to 1928.

The license for this pub can be traced back to the restoration of King Charles II in 1668. Under his seal, an earlier document was renewed, allowing the premises to trade as an inn on this site. The pub is still a warren of nooks, crannies and creaking chairs. You will find good traditional music sessions on Sunday afternoons. A sign in the pub says: 'Only traditional Irish music allowed in this bar'. Long may it last!

RYAN'S
28 PARKGATE STREET, DUBLIN 8

MANY VISITORS will travel west and south by train from the beautifully restored Heuston Station at Kingsbridge. If you are making a trip, be sure to build in an extra half hour to visit Ryan's (stop 18 on the City Tour bus route). When you go through the door you immediately think: 'Thank goodness for the Dublin pub'. This place is a work of art. The old whiskey barrels, the brass taps and the tea drawers are reminiscent of times past. Modern life has crept in too. The flat-screen TV is here and piped music has been introduced for 'atmosphere'. Not even in this gem of a pub can silence be savoured.

The pub – affectionately known as Bongo Ryan's – is a magnificent example of the ecclesiastical style Victorian interior that has retained its snugs and the central carved oak and mahogany bar. The room is served by a three-sided bar that positively gleams when the woodwork is illuminated in the afternoon sunshine. Brass gas lamps and engraved mirrors have made the pub untouchable and thankfully unscathed since it was built in 1896. The two-faced clock that dominates the bar was made by Jacob Frengley, a Dublin clockmaker.

James Fox, a licensed vintner, also ran a hotel at this address in 1870. Michael Hayden carried on the trade until 1921, when he asked his ex-employee William Ryan to buy the pub. According to Thom's directory, the rateable valuation was £95 at that time. The pub was in the Ryan family for seventy-four years. William's grandson John sold it in 1995. Des Buckley, the current owner, bought the pub for more than €2.5 million in 2005. He was wise to keep the old name, as it is lodged firmly in the minds of Irish people as 'the place' to go before a long train journey west or after a stroll in the park. Whiskey connoisseurs will be happy they made the effort to stop here, as the pub boasts over twenty different brands of American, Scotch and Irish whiskies.

In Joyce's *Ulysses* the Viceroy of Ireland, William Humble, and his wife crossed the city along the north quays, passing the pub at 28 Parkgate Street. The king's representative lived in the Phoenix Park and, on 16 June 1904, saluted 'obsequious policemen' on his way into the city. He passed the admiring barmaids of the Ormond Hotel and even Simon Daedalus (Joyce's father), who was crossing the road from a public urinal.

The United States Ambassador's residence is in the Phoenix Park, and so many dignitaries have stopped off at Ryan's to raise a glass. President George Bush (Senior) and Australian Prime Minister Bob Hawke were both served the local brew by John Ryan. 'Mr Bush had a glass of stout and paid for it himself', recalled the owner. Bono and other band members of U2 were regulars and occasionally return there after conquering the home crowd at a concert in the Phoenix Park.

If you are sitting in Ryan's pub on a weekday afternoon, you can still see, hear and smell the Guinness Brewery across the river, but barges no longer pull away eastward towards the docks. The sound and odour of the great institution will continue into the future as Diageo has recently announced that it will not move Guinness's brewery out of the city. The brand is too emotionally attached to Dublin – and vice versa.

THE COBBLESTONE

NORTH KING STREET, DUBLIN 7

THE COBBLESTONE is the last of the many pubs that served the historic Smithfield market. Real music fans will be glad to hear that this traditional market pub is one of the 'in places' for live sounds. It has an excellent mix of traditional, bluegrass, folk and ballad sessions.

Smithfield may be north of the River Liffey and psychologically cut off from the marketing vibe of Temple Bar, but do not let that put you off going there. Millions of euros have been pumped into apartment-building here, to make city-centre living a reality for thousands. The Luas tram line to Tallaght runs through Smithfield and the wide space of the old market has become a haven for strollers, buskers and roller-bladers on the long summer evenings. The renaissance in the area includes the welcome return of the Lighthouse Cinema which screens an eclectic programme of classic and arthouse movies.

The newly refurbished backroom of the Cobblestone has been fitted out with a bar tucked into the corner, allowing for maximum focus on the stage and the excellent music on offer. There is always a buzz in this dark, low-ceilinged pub. This is perhaps because the owners of the Cobblestone are musicians themselves and enthusiastic Irish speakers. The Mulligan family holds the license to trade here now.

The danger with any music venue is mapping it for the mass tourist market. This will not happen in the Cobblestone; it is too small and intimate, and in the safe hands of the purists. You can wander into the front bar and hear anything up to a dozen musicians kicking up a storm. The place is so small that chatting to your neighbours is inevitable. Strangers soon become friends here.

THE OLD STAND

37 EXCHEQUER STREET, DUBLIN 2

THIS GREAT pub is located at the corner of Exchequer Street and St Andrew Street. The street name goes back to the thirteenth century, when the Royal Exchequer was located here. Half the street was renamed in 1837, when the traders of Grafton Street lobbied to have the nearest end called Wicklow Street, to keep in with the upmarket cachet of the area. The name of the pub derives from the demolished stand at Ireland's famous rugby cradle, Lansdowne Road.

In medieval times, St Andrew Street was known as Hog Hill. It ran alongside the earliest Viking parliament, called the Thing Mote (assembly place). The Old Stand was almost the last pub in the city to introduce television in both bars (Neary's on Chatham Street still holds out). The pub was once a grocery store but only alcohol was sold after John Cox took over in 1885.

The most famous patron of the pub was Michael Collins – the man who signed the treaty that created the Irish Free State (and copper fastened the partition of the country). The 'big fellow' was renowned for his disguises and could pass in and out of pubs without being apprehended by the British Authorities, who wanted him for his part in leading the Irish War of Independence (1919–21). He used this pub to gather information about the profiles and whereabouts of many prominent members of the British Secret Service.

The artefacts in both rooms range from the large Welsh dresser in the upper bar to an abundance of horse brasses and a large canopy island in the lower bar. Paintings of Fishamble Street and Blackhall Place are matched with the historic photograph of the funeral of

Kevin O'Higgins, the first minister for Justice in the Irish Free State. He was charged with protecting the fledgling democracy from subversive anti-treaty protesters; this included passing the order to execute many fellow Irishmen during the Civil War of 1922–23. His funeral cortege passed the pub in 1927, when it was called the Monico.

The pub is run by the Doran brothers, Colclough and Michel. They are part of a well-known family of publicans who have been in the Dublin pub trade for over a century. The trade here reflects the business of the area around South William Street and the Market Arcade just up the road. Many of the customers are women, who like to enjoy their food and drink in comfortable surroundings – and that is just what they get in this friendly well-run establishment.

THE INTERNATIONAL BAR

23 WICKLOW STREET, DUBLIN 2

THIS LANDMARK pub stands prominently on the corner of Wicklow Street and hosts some of the best comedians that the city has produced in the last twenty years. The famous Comedy Cellar kicked off in 1988, when Ardal O'Hanlon (Dougal in *Father Ted*) and friends put on sketches and stand-up routines in the hope of attracting an audience. It was slow in coming but others joined in. Now, almost every comedian in Dublin cuts his or her teeth at the Wednesday-night club.

The ground floor pub is dominated by the one-piece reredos (more often seen behind the altar of a church). It is beautifully carved in mahogany and dwarfs the pub. The bar is made from polished granite, although it is no longer partitioned for discreet imbibing. Watch out for the seven wooden figureheads behind the bar — these represent the river gods of Ireland. You can also see the shape of the old whiskey and wine barrels (with the brass taps still in place). From these, the harder liquor was dispensed to customers buying their groceries from Mary Meredith in the early nineteenth century.

The pub has been here for two hundred years. In 1854, the registered license holder was John Dunne. In the 1880s, John Cox exploited the potential of this and the Old Stand across the road, when he took over both premises. John Donoghue is now the proprietor. He believes the pub takes its name from Connolly's Column, which fought as part of the International Brigade in the Spanish Civil War. However, the International Bar is mentioned in James Joyce's *Ulysses*: young Master Dignam, son of the late Paddy, sticks his head into the pub on Bloomsday 1904. The Irish Socialist Brigade held their meetings here before Frank Ryan led almost 200 of them to the Civil War in 1937. When you enter the house, watch out for the mosaic of the letters OD at the entrance: the initials of the family that currently owns the pub. The 1916 Rebellion Walking Tour starts here. See www.1916rising.com.

O'NEILL'S

2 SUFFOLK STREET, DUBLIN 2

THE SPLENDID Victorian exterior attracts visitors and locals to this sturdy old pub. When you walk through the doors, you are in for a pleasant surprise. In the late morning, there are the usual statuesque male figures adding to the stillness, breaking the moment only when they raise a glass to their lips.

O'Neills has much to recommend it, not least the elaborate pub food at the carvery: the portions would satisfy a prizefighter. A maze of rooms beef out this pub. The snug is perfectly positioned away from the bar; it even has its own entrance and serving counter. The pub is popular with all sorts of business types partial to a substantial lunch. The food on offer now competes with sporting moments on TV to attract fickle pub customers.

The landmark corner site has always benefited from the local trade in the area. The old Irish parliament was just down Church Lane on Hoggen Green (now known as College Green). Trinity College was a hop and skip away. The parochial church of Grattan's independent assembly was St Andrew's, which is just across the road. The pub has therefore drawn from wig, town and gown for more than three hundred years.

© Failte Ireland

From 1755 to 1875, the Coleman family held the licence here and enjoyed the custom of the bankers, stockbrokers and accountants who worked in the financial houses nearby. The pub became known as O'Neills in 1927, when the current owners took it over from Paul Hogan, who had made the corner pub a popular place for the purchase of tea, wines, spirits and beer. He ran an orderly house and took no nonsense from the unruly elements of Trinity College.

Many writers have come here, as it stands at the crossing point between Temple Bar and Grafton Street. The northern poet Michael Longley was a regular when he was a Fellow at Trinity College in 1993. Another habitué was the much admired poet and academic Brendan Kennelly (*See* PAGE 11). His doctors eventually cautioned him to stay out of pubs and to stop drinking or he would be dead within a year. The poet replied, 'I had to think long and hard about that because a man can drink a hell of a lot in a year'.

For Kennelly, poetry is the 'ultimate democracy'. He is very much a poet of the people, down to earth and innocent of literary pretensions. If you see him in O'Neills, approach and hear what he has to say; he is quite the raconteur.

Another regular to O'Neills in the 1990s was the Belfast writer Brian Keenan. He had just started teaching in the American University of Beirut when he was taken hostage by the Islamic Jihad. His five years in captivity, along with the British journalist John McCarthy, are brilliantly described in his book *An Evil Cradling*. He completed it while he was writer-in-residence at Trinity College.

THE BANK ON COLLEGE GREEN

20—22 COLLEGE GREEN, DUBLIN 2

WHEN YOU cross the threshold into this stunning pub you will be struck by its fiscal origins. From the beautiful Directors' Room (now serving as a snug) to the old safes on the way downstairs — via a fine marble staircase — the pub has all the hallmarks of solidity and tradition. William Henry Lynn designed this impressive Victorian finance hall. Upon entering the pub you will pass a sign for the Royal Bank, which merged with the Munster & Leinster, and the Provincial to create the biggest single bank in the Irish market. Incredibly, the idea came about at a urinal in the Shelbourne Hotel, where two prominent rivals were attending the Institute of Bankers' annual dinner. In the 'gents', one of them thought it would be a good idea to get together — in the business sense. It was 1966 and the Allied Irish Bank (AIB) was born.

As you enter the pub you will pass a figure of the sports writer Con Houlihan, the most 'busted' man in Ireland. The saying refers to the number of statues that have been erected to him in bars around Dublin. They were 'naturally in pubs, not chapels' he remarked.

This bank was prominent in one financial scandal in the 1990s. At that time you could come into this building and deposit money in a bogus non-resident savings account to avoid paying tax on the interest. The AIB opened these accounts. Their reason for doing so: all the other banks were at it. The scandal broke, many were caught and the Irish taxman netted millions of euros in penalties from the AIB.

The financial heart of Dublin has moved away from College Green to a new hub in the city's docklands. The investor Dermot Desmond came up with the idea and was encouraged by the late Charles

Haughey. In 1979, Haughey owed the AIB over £500,000. When the bank's directors called him in to explain how he proposed to pay back the loan, he reportedly said: 'I think you will find I can be a very troublesome customer'. He became Taoiseach (Prime Minister) soon afterwards.

THE STAG'S HEAD

1 DAME COURT, DUBLIN 2

WHEN LOUIS Fitzgerald bought the beautiful Stag's Head in 2005, he added another landmark building to his portfolio of more

© Failte Ireland

than twenty pubs. Dame Court runs parallel to Dame Street and they are linked by a narrow passageway. Watch out for the mosaic of a stag's head on the pavement on Dame Street (just before the junction with South Great George's Street). In 1769, Dame Street – which was named after the Saint Marie del Dam nunnery – was widened by the Wide Streets Commissioners. You will notice the imposing Central Bank of Ireland, which dwarfs many of the streets of Temple Bar. The building was designed by Sam Stephenson, who also built the rightly pilloried 'bunkers' or Civic Offices for Dublin City Council on Wood Quay.

The Stag's Head is one of the most lavishly designed Victorian gin palaces in the city. The panelling, mirrors and stained glass give the pub a distinctly religious character. The bar is made of mahogany and capped with red Connemara marble. The wonderful partitions complete the churchlike atmosphere that adds to the intimacy of the chat with friend or stranger in this pub.

The Stag's Head was one of the first pubs in Dublin to be fitted with electric lighting. It was designed by architect A. J. McLaughlin in 1895 and its authentic interior has always attracted film and TV companies from around the world. Scenes from *The Treaty* (starring Brendan Gleeson) were filmed here, as was a sequence from *Educating Rita* (starring Michael Caine and Julie Walters). James Joyce knew the pub and drank here occasionally. The real Michael Collins drank here too. The film director Quentin Tarantino turned up here late one evening just as the bar was closing. He was happy to return the next day for lunch.

The elegant snug is reached through a separate entrance at the end of the bar. In Victorian times, this served as a smoking room. It is wood-panelled with many mirrors, which gives a feeling of extra space.

IT'S ALL IN A NAME

PICTORIAL SIGNS — showing hops or brewing implements — hung over the doorway of many pubs. Sometimes the local Lord or landowner was honoured by having the pub named after him, with his coat of arms displayed on the hanging sign. A famous person might also be honoured: Conan Doyle's pub in Phibsboro is named after the great detective writer. In Ireland, the family name was also important, especially when publicans came from the country to the city. Such was the attachment to home and county, village and family that pub names were often those of the original licence holder, showing that ownership was rarely in the hands of breweries or pub chains, as is the case in England.

THE PORTERHOUSE

16—18 PARLIAMENT STREET, DUBLIN 2

THE CONCEPT of the Porterhouse was created in 1989, when cousins Liam La Hart and Oliver Hughes bought an old building in Bray, County Wicklow. Authenticity was foremost in their minds. They wanted to make beer organically and to produce it along traditional lines from the best raw materials: yeast, hops, cereal grains and pure water. Foam enhancers, preservatives and synthetic sweeteners will not augment your pint at the Porterhouse. In the 1980s, the owners had started a brewery called Harty's, and the know-how they gleaned there gave them the edge when they opened a microbrewery at new premises in Temple Bar.

At the beginning of the twentieth century, Griffith & Company ran a hardware store and general merchants at 16–17 Parliament Street; next door, Paul Aitken carried on his trade as a wine and spirit merchant. In 1996, the creators of the Porterhouse made the shrewd move of buying Rumpoles, a pub at 17 Parliament Street. Incidentally, the site housed the original Custom House for Dublin before James Gandon completed his remarkable building on the riverfront in 1791.

In the 1990s, the street was part of what turned out to be a very successful makeover of the western end of Temple Bar, and the new boom flooded onto this once dreary thoroughfare. The owners began brewing beer on the premises but demand from their other outlets – in Covent Garden (in London) and Glasnevin (on the north side of Dublin) – became so great that the whole production process was transferred to Blanchardstown (to the west of the city). The only evidence of the original brewing process is the large copper kettle still on display on the third floor.

The pub is arranged over three levels, and this theme of 'three' continues in the beer: three choices from three types of speciality brews. Tourists and locals have responded to the novelty of the venture. Being open to new tastes, they can now experience a choice of beers which are brewed exclusively for the Porterhouse. The atmosphere is relaxed and the décor traditional, with wooden floors, and heavy oak tables and benches reminiscent of a small brewer's pub of long ago.

Branches at 45–47 Nassau Street, Dublin 2; Cross Guns Bridge, Glasnevin, Dublin 9; Strand Road, Bray, County Wicklow; and 21–22 Maiden Lane, London WC2.

FARRINGTON'S
28 EAST ESSEX STREET, DUBLIN 2

THIS PUB occupies the corner of East Essex Street and Eustace Street and is named after one of the characters in Joyce's short story 'Counterparts' in *Dubliners*. It is a great stopping off point when exploring the west end of Temple Bar. Dubliners over thirty will remember the Norseman on the same spot. It was owned and run by the benevolent John Morris (who gave financial aid and a sympathetic ear to many an artist and actor working in the area). At that time, there was just the main bar. However, like many other premises in the area, it has been doubled in size by expansion into the building next door.

Nobody in Dublin will remember the pub as J. J. O'Neill's, as it was known in Joyce's time. In 'Counterparts', the central character Farrington enters the pub and skips downstairs to the toilets. He does a pub crawl of his own, which comes to an end in Mulligan's of Poolbeg Street. Theatrical folk have long flocked to the pub after opening nights at the Project Theatre just down the road.

Eustace Street, which runs south from the pub, was named after Sir Maurice Eustace, the speaker of the House of Commons in 1639. Both he and the Duke of Ormond created the Phoenix Park. The most interesting building in the street is perhaps the Irish Film Centre. This had been a Quaker meeting place since 1692, and the main cinema is housed in the original hall. The rear of the building opens out onto Meeting House Square, which is a wonderful public space. On Saturdays, an organic food market takes over the square and is avidly supported by visitors and locals. Films are shown in the square during the summer (and these are free). The Gallery of Photography has an entrance from the square and exhibits works of Irish and international interest.

The cobbled streets of Temple Bar date back to the seventeenth century. Essex Street was famous for its coffee houses a century later. The citizens of Dublin crossed the city by ferry at two points here before Carlisle Bridge – later renamed O'Connell Bridge – was erected in 1795. One ferry point was at the Bagnio Slip. There was a primitive red light district here – close enough for the frisky young men of Trinity College, who romped and roared through the town, but far enough from home for those older men who needed to be discrete.

Moving along the central spine of Temple Bar you pass the crowds enjoying Dublin's own *Rive Gauche*. The Irish Stock Exchange was housed in a beautiful building at 24–28 Anglesea Street until it closed in 2000, when electronic trading took over. All of Dame Street teemed with life after it was widened in the eighteenth century. Stockbrokers, financial agents and solicitors all plied their trade in what was the banking centre of Dublin. The atmosphere on Dame Street has now been distorted by a glut of anonymous superpubs and convenience stores that add a layer of dinginess to this once majestic thoroughfare.

THE FOGGY DEW
A SONG THAT INSPIRED A PUB'S NAME

All ballads are living ghosts and long for a living voice.

Brendan Kennelly

It was down by the glen one Easter morn
To city fair rode I
Those armoured men in their marching lines
In a squadron passed me by

No Pipes did hum no battle drum
Did sound its loud tattoo
But the Angeles bell o'er the Liffey swell
Rang out in the foggy dew

Arthur Griffith

PALACE BAR

21 FLEET STREET, DUBLIN 2

THIS BEAUTIFUL gin palace, which dates from 1880, is regarded as the holy grail of literary pubs. Along with Ryan's of Parkgate Street, it is one the best preserved pubs in the city. It is often said that when tourists discover a traditional boozer, it is no longer a real pub. This cannot be said about the Palace. There are many pubs of this kind in England but you will no longer find one like this, without the jukebox and gambling machine.

© Failte Ireland

At one time, Fleet Street formed the boundary of the River Liffey on the southside and continued along what is now Temple Bar. The name derives from the old English word 'fleot' (meaning creek or inlet). It became known as Fleet Street in 1685 and, like its English counterpart, was favoured as a place where gentlemen of the *fourth estate* gathered. The *Irish Times* newspaper was printed on this street until 2006. The Palace and Bowes (at 31 Fleet Street) retained a close association with this 'paper of record'. Kevin Barry, the first Republican to be executed during the War of Independence, was born at 8 Fleet Street.

Bertie Smyllie, the larger-than-life editor of the *Irish Times*, would come into the Palace after a brisk cycle ride from Malahide into the city. Smyllie was the king of the Palace. The atmosphere in the pub was often festive with conversation, and blue with pipe tobacco smoke. He insisted on a books page for the newspaper, even when newsprint was rationed during the war — and the *Irish Times* was down to four pages. He created space for writers to get published; he paid them too.

© Failte Ireland

Poets, painters, novelists and playwrights mixed with civil servants, lawyers and hangers-on in this European *café litteraire*. Look closely at the framed photos in the back room and you will notice that many men wore a hat and sucked on a pipe for effect. Among the many well preserved features in the pub is the five-cornered snug; it is one of the cosiest in Dublin. You can even book it and lock the door for complete privacy.

Brian O'Nolan, the finest satirical writer that Ireland produced in the twentieth century, drank here, too often for his own health. He was widely regarded as Joyce's intellectual equal. As a novelist, he wrote under the name of Flann O'Brien. Although they never met, Joyce had a well-thumbed copy of O'Brien's *At Swim Two Birds* among his collection of books.

O'Brien retained the undergraduate's love of jollification and the mischievous prank. On one famous occasion, he borrowed a car without an engine. He parked it outside the pub (having pushed it there) and then pretended to be drunk. He was charged with driving a mechanically propelled vehicle 'while under the influence'. As the car did not have an engine, the charge had to be dropped.

Bertie Smyllie left the Palace when cheques that he cashed there were indiscreetly returned to him with the pub stamp on the back. The editor of such an august publication did not like his bank manager knowing that much of his finances were funnelled through a public house. The 'cultured' Pearl bar (also on Fleet Street) was happy to handle the matter more discretely, and so Smyllie's court gradually transferred its business away from the Palace. The Pearl was never as suitable, though. According to Tony Gray (in his book *Mr Smyllie, Sir*), the pub was u-shaped and thus divided the gatherings, sometimes into hostile camps. When the rival McDaid's

The Palace: renowned for its 'intellectual refreshment'

© Failte Ireland

(in Harry Street) took on the mantle of a literary pub, Smyllie's position in Dublin's intellectual life diminished. He even took to wearing a beret instead of the famous broad-brimmed hat.

The death of James Joyce in 1941 meant that Flann O'Brien lost one of his heroes. In his memoir, *Remembering How We Stood*, John Ryan recalls how Joyce's passing was received by one non-literary publican near Blackrock. He quizzed O'Brien about his sombre demeanour, and was told that the writer James Joyce was dead. The publican was shocked: 'Little Jimmy Joyce, the sign writer, sure wasn't he only sitting on that stool there on Wednesday last week'. Three of the great writers who frequented the Palace died within as many years of each other (Kavanagh and Behan were the other two). Flann O'Brien passed away on April Fools' Day 1966.

GIN PALACES

THE FIRST gin palaces in Britain and Ireland were built in the 1820s. These 'dram shops' began as chemist shops. Gin had medicinal qualities and was sold in the shop to 'take away' or to drink 'standing up' on the premises. Changes in legislation led to these gin palaces becoming larger and requiring licences to sell ale and wine. The fixtures and fittings were lavish (quite gaudy to some eyes), with lighting supplied through ornate new gas lamps (Neary's in Chatham Street is one example). The bar in many Victorian pubs is based on the shop counter of the original gin palace; the service was swift and the counter was ideal for attaching beer pumps.

JOHN MULLIGAN

8 POOLBEG STREET, DUBLIN 2

WHEN DUBLINERS return to their city, they often make a pilgrimage to Mulligan's. This pub, which is surrounded by high-rise buildings noted for their ugliness, is a shrine for the drinker of stout. Leopold Bloom wondered why the black stuff tasted so poor outside Ireland: 'They say the sea air sours it'. This is not the case in Mulligan's.

You will find all generations paying homage to the 'best pint in the best pub in Dublin'. It is difficult to argue with that claim. If pub culture were to die out in Ireland, this would be the last place to turn out the lights. The Society for the Preservation of the Dublin Accent meets here. Just as well too. Sean O'Casey would turn in his grave if he heard the warped Anglo-American accent used by a new generation of Dubliners. Their rugger-bugger brogue is deliciously sent up by Paul Howard in his weekly column in the *Irish Times*: Ross O'Carroll-Kelly.

In 1854, John Mulligan leased the premises for the equivalent of €20 a year. It was a good location. Big ships were able to moor in

© Fáilte Ireland

the deep water nearby, so dockers made up a large proportion of the clientele. Traders at the old Corn Exchange also wet their whistles in the pub.

Characters from the 'Counterparts' story in James Joyce's *Dubliners* turned up here at the tail end of a pub crawl, when the Scotch House was closed. Farrington, O'Halloran and Leonard sat in the back lounge of the pub and noticed a group of performers from the 4,000-seat Theatre Royal just across the road. One of them, a flirtatious dancer, leads Farrington on a wild goose chase of the heart, teasing him to frustration. He goes home and turns violent on one of his children. The story ends with his young son pleading: 'Don't beat me, pa! And I'll…I'll say a *Hail Mary* for you'.

The Cavan-born Cusack brothers, Con and Tommy, became the guardians of Mulligan's when they secured it from their uncle, Mick Smyth, who had bought the house from John Mulligan in 1932. They have seen this former working man's pub morph into the trendy haunt of tourists, journalists, sportsmen and literati.

The Who's Who of Ireland and beyond have gathered here over the decades. John F. Kennedy savoured the brews back in 1945, when he worked with Hearst newspapers. The world of theatre was also represented here. Those who starred in the Theatre Royal loved the pub: Jimmy O'Dea, Peggy Dell, Cecil Sheridan, Jack Cruise and Eamonn Andrews are all remembered by the older theatre-going audiences.

For many years, the pub was the favoured haunt of reporters from the *Irish Press* – it was next door. Michael O'Toole, the features editor, remembered how Flann O'Brien regarded copy for submission to that newspaper: it had to have the imprimatur of a porter stain (probably stamped in Mulligan's). If none existed, the chief sub-editor would spike the piece!

In 1931, Eamon De Valera founded the *Irish Press* to echo his view of Irishness. In 1954, the *Evening Press* was launched, and so three national newspapers (including the *Sunday Press*) were produced right beside Mulligan's. De Valera's ideal of an Irish Ireland was reflected in the editorial pronouncements of the *Irish Press*. However, all three titles failed to change as the country became increasingly urbanised and the newspaper's rural readership shrank. Publication ceased in 1995.

There are no psychedelic innovations in Mulligan's. The whole effect is sombre and traditional, and the colour scheme subdued. There is an abundance of Victorian counter tops and mahogany, with plenty of confessional screens, dark corners, and crevices – ideal for intimacy, gossip and pints of creamy porter. Slip through the narrow door into the lounge, where you will see a collection of old theatrical posters, recapturing the great days of the Theatre Royal, which was closed down and demolished in 1962. Sample the spirit of this great Dublin institution, its calmness during the day, and its buzz in the evening. Join the inoffensive looking guy consuming brandy and milk – that might be Con Houlihan. He, like Kavanagh, can 'still stroke the monsters back or write with un-poisoned pen'.

KENNEDY'S

31—32 WESTLAND ROW, DUBLIN 2

IN 1870, Thom's directory listed John McGauran as a grocer and wine merchant at 31–32 Westland Row. By 1931, the pub was in the hands of W. & M. Kennedy; at that time, the rateable valuation was £145.00. Dubliners remember this pub as Kenney's in the 1990s.

According to Thomas Cleary (the current owner), this was because the letter 'd' had simply fallen off the name! He warmly repeats the folklore that a teenaged Oscar Wilde stacked shelves here when the pub served as a grocery store for the hired help of Merrion Square. When asked for proof, he quipped, 'I don't have any payslips to show you'.

The 'Fag on the crag'   © Failte Ireland

Kennedy's is a solid oak-panelled pub, partitioned for cosiness and bolstered by a tasty choice of dishes at lunchtime. There is a nod and wink to all the literati that paced along the pavements outside. The current owner has served some of the modern luminaries, including Seamus Heaney. Indeed, he exhibits quite a nice etching of the Nobel Laureate in the lounge.

Along with the Lincoln Inn, this pub was a regular stop for Samuel Beckett. He lived just around the corner at 6 Clare Street – he had accommodation on the top floor of what was his father's chartered surveying business. His first novel, *More Pricks than Kicks*, was brewed there and some of his later works, including the novel *Murphy*, were incubating at the same address. It was a time of isolation for the writer, who was down on his luck. In 1938, he made a complete break with Ireland by 'returning home' to Paris.

Kennedy's makes a great stop-off point before the onward journey to Oscar Wilde's birthplace on Westland Row, or a visit to his monument ('the fag on the crag') just across from his parents' house at 1 Merrion Square. You will pass what was the Merrion Hall Protestant Church. The façade from 1863 remains, integrated into the Davenport Hotel on Lower Merrion Street. Samuel Beckett and George Bernard Shaw both furthered their education with constant visits to the National Gallery, which is just around the corner. There are now two entrances to the exhibition halls – via the magnificent Millennium Wing on Clare Street and the more formal access through the Dargan Wing on Merrion Square. As a gesture of appreciation, Shaw directed that the royalties of *Pygmalion* and *My Fair Lady* should go to the National Gallery – a bequest that continues until 2020.

In *Ulysses*, Stephen Dedalus turns the corner from Lincoln Place to Westland Row and passes the pub when James Conway was trading here in 1904. The 'literary turk' was on his way to the Monto (*See* PAGE 146) , where 'shady Mary' worked. Joyce traces his steps to here from the National Maternity Hospital in an episode called *Oxen of the Sun*. Dedalus, Bloom and other characters had been drinking in Burke's pub, on the corner of Fenian Street and Holles Street (this is now a flower shop).

THE SHELBOURNE

27 ST STEPHEN'S GREEN, DUBLIN 2

What would Dublin do without the Shelbourne hotel?

Oliver St John Gogarty

THE SHELBOURNE Hotel is one of the most enduring institutions in Dublin life. It is named after the Marquees of Shelbourne, and it is up there with the grandest of places to stay. It was established by Martin Burke (a Tipperary man) in 1824, when St Stephen's Green was still a grazing field for the Lord Mayor's cattle. Access to the square was originally by a laneway, which is now Grafton Street.

Society in the ascendant has always met here. Deals have been sealed on the mezzanine floor, captains of industry have been

'adiosed' in the deep green damask of the Constitution Room and swanky wedding parties have arrived, windswept, into the foyer.

For two years, Dubliners had to do without the 'Shelbo' and its glitzy cachet. A major renovation began in 2005 and was completed in April 2007, at a cost of more than €40 million. It certainly needed one. The floors had become so uneven that the food trolleys were known to roll off on a frolic of their own. The 'Queen on the Green' was last refurbished in the 1860s by John McCurdy, who designed the pillared entrance and graceful staircase. This time, the chandeliers and the Georgian furniture are back and the place is set to swing once more.

William Thackeray stayed here and, according to his *Irish Sketchbook* of 1843, he paid over six shillings for full board. He ordered a broiled Dublin Bay herring for breakfast when he heard the fish seller passing the door, melodiously marketing her wares. The writer mused about whether you would find anything as tasty in the Bay of Naples: 'Dolphins perhaps but they are better off in a sonnet than on the breakfast table'.

When the social season mattered, the city's folk came to hunt balls and weddings at the hotel. The writer Elizabeth Bowen remarks in her memoir *Seven Winters* that ordinary citizens gathered outside the hotel to 'get a goo' at who was coming and going. Dubliners still do that – but from the inside. You can jostle for position with celebs and hangers on in the Horseshoe Bar, where 'women with a past met men with no future'.

Bowen found the grandeur of it all extreme: from the gleam of the satin gowns to the jewellery catching the rays of the evening sun. You can still hear the clop-clop of the horse and carriage passing by but without the pomp and splendour of those years. The hotel became the destination for the visiting Anglo-Irish, who were tucked away in their 'granite boxes' outside the capital. The hotel was convenient for the social whirl and stodgy pomp that revolved around Dublin Castle, the Spring Show and the Horse Show.

When the shooting started on Easter Monday 1916, tea could no longer be served to the ladies of Dublin in the front drawing room. Stray bullets knocked the tops off flowers in the vases nearby. Eventually, the hotel was garrisoned by the British army and sandbags were erected in front of the bay windows. Army snipers took up positions on the roof and traded bullets with the rebels stationed in St Stephen's Green. The writer James Stephens took refuge here during the Rising and recorded the week's events in his eyewitness account, *The Insurrection in Dublin*. He tells how women from Baggot Street stayed up all night serving tea and bread to the soldiers near the hotel.

There have been many famous guests here, including Princess Grace of Monaco, Luciano Pavarotti, John F and Jackie Kennedy, Harold Wilson, Stan Laurel, Rock Hudson, James Cagney, Richard Burton, Rita Hayworth, John Hurt, Maureen O'Hara, Julia Roberts and Pierce Brosnan. Peter O'Toole was a regular, and once famously bathed in champagne when he stayed.

The writers Brendan Behan and Patrick Kavanagh hung out here, while Seamus Heaney has mingled with the new generation of scribes at the hotel. Bram Stoker lived around the corner at 30 Kildare

Street, and George Moore had rooms on Ely Place. Irish politicians visiting the Shelbourne included Charles Stuart Parnell, Michael Collins and Arthur Griffith, who drafted the Constitution of the Irish Free State here in 1922.

Journalists, politicians, barristers and 'beauty queens in blond helmets' vie for the limelight in the famous Horseshoe Bar (designed in 1958 by the late Sam Stephenson) or skulk around the ground floor corridors. Celebrities are interviewed in the Lord Mayor's lounge over afternoon tea, with cakes stacked high above dainty sandwiches, presented in the style of our colonial masters. You can earwig on the goings-on and then double check what the 'celeb' said in every Sunday newspaper. Indeed, loitering is not frowned upon in the Shelbourne – it is almost encouraged. So do not be afraid to walk into the hotel as if you own it.

Inside you will find paintings by Irish artists like Louis Le Brocquy, Tony O'Malley and Barrie Cooke. Patrons leaving the hotel will pass between the watchful eyes of the Egyptian princesses who have held two lamps aloft since 1867. Guests will come and go past these observant eyes but history still hangs in the corridors and ceilings of this great institution. Nowhere else in Dublin is the buzz, gossip and laughter so intense.

A LITERARY & HISTORICAL
WALK THROUGH THE GREEN

Dublin can be heaven
With coffee at eleven
And a stroll in Stephen's Green

WALKING THROUGH Lord Ardilaun's garden, or St Stephen's
Green, the visitor will be surprised by the number of writers and
political figures honoured there in bronze and stone. The first of
these is just inside the gate on the south side, opposite Newman
House, which was once the old Catholic University of Ireland.
James Joyce is facing his 'sombre college' in a bust designed by
Marjorie Fitzgibbon. The sculpture was unveiled in 1982 to
commemorate the hundredth anniversary of the writer's birth.
The quotation on the plinth is from *A Portrait of the Artist*, when the
hero is 'crossing Stephen's, that is, my green'.

John Henry Newman acquired Clanwilliam House (on the south side of St Stephen's Green) in 1864. He had opened his Catholic University ten years before, as a direct riposte by the Catholic hierarchy to the 'godless' Queen's colleges that had been set up in 1845. The hierarchy must have been gratified at the choice of building for the new college, as Richard 'Buck' Whaley (a previous owner) had said that 'no papist would ever cross the threshold'. The poet Gerard Manly Hopkins was perhaps the most famous Jesuit to teach there. He lived in the house from 1884 until his death from typhoid fever in 1889.

The four sides of this beautiful park were once called Beaux Walk, Leeson's Walk, Monk's Walk and French Walk — French because many Huguenots lived on the less fashionable west side. W. B. Yeats has a stepped garden named after him — this is close to the 'garden for the blind' next to the pond. In 1967, the sculptor Henry Moore created the brooding figure of Yeats entitled 'Knife Edge'. Sir Walter Scott paid a visit to Dublin and dined at 9 St Stephen's Green. In a letter to the novelist Maria Edgeworth, he described the city as 'splendid beyond compare'.

James Joyce

The statue of Robert Emmet — recently moved inside the railings on the westside — remains a symbolic figure for Irish republicans. This sculpture is a replica of a monument in Washington DC that was unveiled by Woodrow Wilson in 1917. In 1803, Emmet fired a 'pale green shot' against the Crown from outside a pub in South Great George's Street. He led a regiment of drunks, none of whom could keep a secret. A botched attempt to seize public buildings, including Dublin Castle, descended into a general riot. Emmet called off the rebellion and fled into hiding in Rathfarnham. The

uprising landed him before a military tribunal, where he was tried and convicted of treason. He was hanged and beheaded outside St Catherine's Church in Thomas Street. Visitors should stop there for a moment and reflect on his speech from the dock:

Let no man write my epitaph; for as no man who knows my motives dares now vindicate them, let not prejudice or ignorance asperse them. When my country takes her place among the nations of the earth, then and not till then, let my epitaph be written.

Emmet's oratory became a byword for students of the law. One of the judges at his trial was moved to tears by the speech. Abraham Lincoln learnt it by heart. Although nobody found his body, Irish republicans have taken ownership of Emmet's words and will write his epithet only when Ireland is reunited into a nation of thirty-two counties. He has gone down in folk memory, with songs and poems sung and recited in pubs all over Dublin – songs that 'bandage up history' as Eavan Boland pointed out:

> *Oh breathe not his name! Let it sleep in the shade,*
> *Where cold and unhonoured his relics are laid!*
>
> Thomas Moore

> *Bold Robert Emmet, the darling of Ireland,*
> *Bold Robert Emmet will die with a smile,*
> *Farewell companions both loyal and daring,*
> *I'll lay down my life for the Emerald Isle.*
>
> Anon

Traitors' Gate – the grand entrance to St Stephen's Green at the top of Grafton Street – commemorates the Royal Dublin Fusiliers and records their bravery in the Boer War. Just inside the gate is a lump of Wicklow granite. This monument symbolizes the unquenchable spirit of Jeremiah O'Donovan Rossa, the Fenian patriot who founded the Phoenix Movement in 1858 (later known as the Irish Republican Brotherhood). He remained closely involved in the rebranding of Irish nationalism

until his death in 1915, at the age of eighty-four. Irish republicans instantly recognized his passing for its propaganda value. Patrick Pearse (author of the 1916 Proclamation) seized the moment in a famous graveside oration at Rossa's funeral in Glasnevin Cemetery:

> *Life springs from death; and from the graves of patriot men and women spring living nations. The defenders of this Realm have worked well in secret and in the open. They think that they have pacified Ireland. They think that they have purchased half of us and intimidated the other half. They think that they have foreseen everything, think that they have provided against everything; but, the fools, the fools, the fools! They have left us our Fenian dead, and while Ireland holds these graves, Ireland unfree shall never be at peace.*

The bronzed bust of James Clarence Mangan (designed by Oliver Sheppard in 1909) stands pensively in the central circle of the park. The figure of 'Dark Rosaleen' that resides in the niche of the pedestal was the last work of the sculptor Willie Pearse, brother

James Clarence Mangan

of Patrick Pearse. Mangan, the son of a grocer, was born in Christchurch Place in 1803. He is noted for his poetry and journalism and particularly as the writer of the ballad *Dark Rosaleen*. In keeping with nineteenth-century tradition, this song personified the nation as a woman:

Oh My Dark Rosaleen,
Do not sigh, do not weep!
The priests are on the ocean green,
They march along the deep.
There's wine from the royal Pope,
Upon the ocean green;
And Spanish ale shall give you hope,
My Dark Rosaleen!
My own Rosaleen!

Mangan began to contribute to the *Nation* newspaper, founded by Thomas Davis in 1842. Joyce held the poet in high regard, although he did not like to acknowledge the influence of any other Irish author. Yeats was also impressed: 'To the soul of Clarence Mangan was tied the burning ribbon of genius', he said. Mangan was a regular of the Bleeding Horse in Camden Street and the Phoenix Tavern in D'Olier Street. In Dublin, he was known for his bloodless, corpselike features, dyed blond hair and regular intake of opium. He cut a dash on the city's streets with 'his odd little cloak, and wonderful hat ... his flax-coloured wig and false teeth ... wearing a huge pair of dark green spectacles'. He lived most of his life in poverty and died from the combined effects of malnutrition, brought on by alcohol abuse, and cholera in the Meath hospital in 1849.

Close to Mangan in the central circle is a bust of Countess Markievicz. She came from the Gore-Booth family in County Sligo and was a major in the Irish Citizens' Army. She was sentenced to death for her involvement in the Easter Rising but, because of her gender, she was sent instead to a 'university of revolution' (a British gaol). In 1918, she represented Sinn Féin in the General Election, and was the first woman to be elected to the British House of Commons (she refused to take her seat). Sean O'Casey, who knew her, said: 'One thing she had in abundance was physical courage; with that she was clothed as with a garment'.

Countess Markievicz

GEORGE MOORE'S IMPRESSION OF ST STEPHEN'S GREEN (FROM *HAIL AND FAREWELL*)

THE FIRST thing I saw on entering the Green was a girl loosening her hair to the wind, and, following her down a sunny alley, I found myself suddenly by a brimming lake, curving like some wonderful calligraphy round a thickly planted headland, the shadows of some great elms reflected in the water, and the long, young leaves of the willow sweeping the surface.

I went in quest of new interests, finding one in an equestrian statue that ornamented the centre of the Green. There were parterres of flowers about it, and in the shade, people of all ages sat half asleep, half awake, enjoying the spring morning like myself. I wandered on, enchanted by the going and coming of the sun, one moment implanting a delicious warmth between my shoulder-blades, and at the next leaving me cold, forgetful of Yeats until I saw him in his black cloak striding in a green alley.

Thomas Kettle

Thomas Kettle (whose statue stands on the east side of the central circle) was a poet, barrister and MP for East Tyrone. He edited the *Nationalist* newspaper and joined the Irish Volunteers in 1913. He fought with the Royal Dublin Fusiliers in World War One. Kettle was devastated by the news of the Rising of 1916: 'They have ruined it all, the dream of a free united Ireland in a free Europe'. He died in the battle of Guinchy in September 1916.

Like Patrick Pearse, Kettle contemplates Ireland's history. His poem *Reason in Rhyme* ends with a plea to the English not to forget the past:

We keep the past for pride:
No deepest peace shall strike our poets dumb:
No rawest squad of all Death's volunteers,

No rudest man who died
To tear your flag down in the bitter years,
But shall have praise, and three times thrice again,
When at the table men shall drink with men.

The northeast gateway to the park is notable for the Wolfe Tone memorial, designed by Edward Delaney. The bronze statue is framed by a granite screen wall, behind which is a sculpture entitled 'Famine'. Wolfe Tone, the father of Irish Republicanism, slit his throat with a penknife rather than face the hangman's noose for treason after the 1798 Rebellion.

His statue is rather more robust than a contemporary description of him by John Walsh, a Trinity student, who later became Attorney General of Ireland. In 1791, he attended a meeting of the United Irishmen in Tailor's Hall (known then as the Back Lane Parliament):

Theobald Wolfe Tone

I walked in and found the society in full debate. I saw there, for the first time, the men with the three names. The first [Tone] was a slightly effeminate looking man, with a hatchet face, a long aquiline nose, rather handsome and genteel-looking, with lank, straight hair combed down on his sickly red cheek, exhibiting a face the most insignificant and mindless that could be imagined. I set him down as a worthy, good-natured, flimsy man, in whom there was no harm.

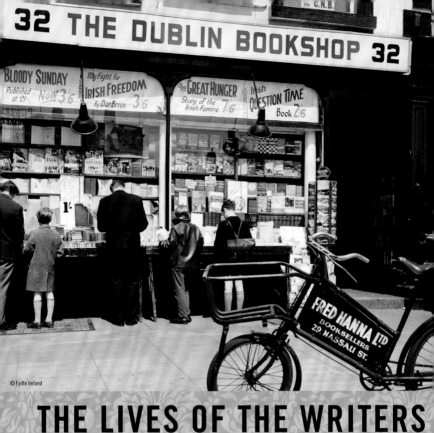

© Failte Ireland

THE LIVES OF THE WRITERS

HISTORICAL BACKGROUND

For the newcomer or tourist Ireland is simply charming,
but it is also an old island, full of demons and old hate

Iris Murdoch

YOU CAN take the writer out of Dublin but you cannot take Dublin out of the writer. The Irish XI is sure to feature strongly in any anthology of the great white male writers of the twentieth century. Many of them did have a love of sport – Beckett for cricket and horseracing, and Behan for soccer, but not Shaw for golf. Many Irish writers rejected the four 'F' words of Irish life – faith, fatherland, family and friendship – and left the country. Joyce took the lead and moved to mainland Europe 'to forge in the smithy of my soul the uncreated conscience of my race'.

A string of literary talent had emerged in Ireland from 1890 onward. It gravitated towards the ascendancy houses of Ireland – those 'ships out at sea' – and their more humble abodes in Georgian Dublin. Like many artistic movements, this one began with a group of expatriates. In April 1892, W.B. Yeats gathered his friends in Chiswick in London to establish the Irish Literary Society. Within a year, Douglas Hyde, first President of Ireland, founded the influential Gaelic League. This organisation pledged to preserve and revive Irish as the vernacular.

It all happened in Dublin. George Moore called the city 'the capital of the Celtic Renaissance'. The Irish Literary Theatre was opened in 1899 and the Abbey came into existence five years later. What emerged was a movement to revive the native language, arts and crafts. In the tearooms of Dublin, the talk was of Irish renewal based on the rich lore and traditions of the past.

However, the Literary Revival began to break down when the leaders argued and fell out. In 1928, the Abbey Theatre rejected Sean O'Casey's *The Silver Tassie*, and so he left Ireland, vowing not to return. He had done for the Dublin working class what Synge had done for the rural Irish peasant: he gave them a voice. He did not, however, expect it to be silenced by the National Theatre.

For many writers, Dublin was a provincial backwater – priest-ridden, parochial and paralysed. Joyce called it 'the seventh city of Christendom' and it was not a place that encouraged free artistic expression – quite the contrary. In 1926, the Irish government set up a committee to investigate the 'evil literature' found in English magazines and newspapers. When the Censorship of Publications Act was passed in 1929, its reach was felt into the area of published books that were deemed 'indecent or obscene'.

Very few contemporary writers escaped rebuke. Even in the relatively relaxed period from 1960 to 1965, some 1,900 books were banned – an average of about thirty a month. The five-man censorship committee included a representative of the Catholic Church. 'Christ and Caesar worked hand in glove' to prevent the 'Californication' of Irish life. The puritanical Irish – 'Paddy Stink and Micky Mud' – as Joyce dubbed them – were content with one form of national identity: Gaelic-speaking and Catholic, nationalist and anti-English.

In this atmosphere, writers were impoverished. In 1940, Patrick Kavanagh left the 'stony grey soil' of County Monaghan and came to Dublin. He walked part of the hundred miles to get here. The city was not forgiven for leaving him in poverty. Kavanagh took part in the second literary renaissance that flourished after the Second World War – the 'skin head' brigade. The first literary flowering took place around the Big Houses of Anglo Ireland, but the second wave flourished in pubs frequented by journalists. It became an underground movement, hidden from official Ireland.

When the Second World War broke out, many Irish intellectuals agreed with DeValera's neutral position for this fledgling democracy: that the new state could ill afford to spend slender resources on a prolonged fight against fascism. The isolation that followed cut many writers off from the outside world. Economically, the country was a 'basket case'. DeValera's vision of frugal self-sufficiency ensured one thing: mass emigration to 'pagan England' and elsewhere. Many younger Irish women were to leave rather than enter an arranged loveless marriage with an older man waiting for the bequest of land by right of being the first-born. Edna O'Brien portrays that young, fallible, flesh-and-blood woman in her work, notably *The Country Girls*.

The new gang of writers poured into pubs like McDaid's and the Palace Bar. They were endowed with a conspiratorial glamour. Each of them had a problem with alcohol; he could never get enough of it.

The central figure was Brendan Behan – a painter, republican, singer and 'drinker with a writing problem'. He was the first Irish

© Failte Ireland

writer to be 'discovered' by television, and he was quite the performer. Malcolm Muggeridge and the BBC will not forget him. When he was shown into the green room of the BBC studios in Shepherd's Bush, he spotted a bottle of whiskey on a table. 'I had no option but to drink the lot', he said. He went on TV to do the live chat show and used the 'F' word liberally throughout. Wherever Behan went, journalists lay in wait. When he arrived in 'Presbyterian Toronto' he was asked about the purpose of his visit: 'I'm here to drink Canada dry', he said. (The quip made reference to Canada Dry, a brand of mixer for drinks.)

The political, economic and artistic climate began to change in 1959. Eamon DeValera gave way to a new man with an entrepreneurial vision: Sean Lemass. He saw Ireland as a country of ambition and wealth. It was to be a place where multi-national corporations were welcome. In the new decade, over 350 foreign companies came to Ireland to manufacture and trade. People flocked back home. Emigration was reduced to a trickle. Society opened up. Television played its part here, and allowed traditional orthodoxy to be challenged. Consumerism was born. In 1967, books that had been banned for twelve years could now be read.

The subject of sex could now be more openly discussed. Officially, it did not exist until television arrived. One politician even remarked: 'There was no sex in Ireland before television'. From Joyce at one end of the twentieth century to Emma Donoghue at the other, the preoccupation is clear. Both writers vividly recount their sexual awakening – albeit from very different perspectives. Joyce's came in the 'Monto' (the red light district of Dublin) at the turn of the century. He succumbed to a young prostitute who, he recalled, in *A Portrait of the Artist*, was both leisurely and perfumed:

> *He surrendered himself to her, body and mind, conscious of nothing in the world but the dark pressure of her softly parting lips...and between them he felt an unknown and timid pressure, darker than the swoon of sin, softer than sound or odour.*

It is interesting to compare Joyce's experience with the modern novelist Emma Donoghue, who describes her sexual awakening as a lesbian. In her book *Stir Fry* (published in 1994), she observes two of her girlfriends making love on the kitchen table:

> *She couldn't help but see the shape they made...there was no wild passion; that might have shaken her less. Just the slow bartering of lips on the rickety table where Ruth chopped garlic...two friends of hers kissing on the table she ate at every night. Rapt faces and library books and garlic.*

A POETS' COUNCIL

IN 1980, Taoiseach Charles Haughey funded the creation of Aos Dana. This 'poets' council' would be self governing and self elected (without political interference) and would allow its members a basic income. Many sought membership, and 215 were admitted. Although Charles Haughey was shown to be one of the most corrupt politicians in the country, he was also a champion of the writer and artist in Irish society. He helped to return them to official patronage, in the way that the *file* (poet) was a protected and necessary appointee in older Gaelic society (before 1600). There are currently 226 members (the ceiling is 250). Each member resident in Ireland gets a grant (*cnuas*) of just over €11,000 for five years, which is renewable at the discretion of the Arts Council.

SAMUEL BECKETT (1906–1989)

There's man all over for you, blaming on his boots the fault of his feet
Waiting for Godot

SAMUEL BECKETT was born into a well-to-do Protestant family in Foxrock, County Dublin in 1906. He attended Portora Royal College in Enniskillen. In 1923, he entered Trinity College, where he excelled at cricket, tennis, golf and even boxing.

He graduated in 1927, winning the gold medal as the first-placed student in his year. He was then awarded a scholarship to live in Paris, where he taught at the Ecole Normale Supérieure. In 1930, he returned to Dublin and began lecturing in French at Trinity College. He lasted only four terms, resigning because he could not bear to teach others what he did not fully understand himself. He was to divide his time between Dublin, 'the intellectual fog' of London, and Paris, where he finally settled in 1938: 'France at war is more interesting

© Failte Ireland

than Ireland at peace', he noted. He also gave up on the English language, preferring to write in French: 'English gives me too many opportunities for the stylist. In French you can write without style'.

Beckett had a long and productive friendship with fellow expatriate James Joyce. Joyce's failing sight gave Beckett the opportunity to assist him in a number of ways, acting as his secretary and researching sections of Joyce's extravagant *Finnegan's Wake*. Beckett later observed that Joyce was the great marshaller of information, bringing any detail into his work. In contrast, he was an analyser, trying to leave out as much as he could. Their relationship cooled when he did not return the affections of Joyce's mentally unstable daughter, Lucia.

While studying at Trinity College between 1923 and 1927, Beckett had ample opportunity to observe the traditions of vaudeville, and silent movies. His celluloid heroes were Buster Keaton and Charles Chaplin. These were to influence him while he wrote his most celebrated play, *Waiting for Godot*. Much of the knockabout comedy in the drama rests on the clownish antics of the central characters, Vladimir (Didi) and Estragon (Gogo). His setting is sparse enough: 'A country road. A tree. Evening.'

Beckett was notoriously diffident when it came to talking about his work. However, in an interview for the *New York Post*, he said that much of the dialogue in *Waiting for Godot* was based on daily conversations with his partner, Suzanne, when they were in hiding in the south of France during the Second World War. In the play, Didi and Gogo tell each other jokes and try to recall their past to offset the boredom of daily life. Monsieur Godot never arrives. This is somewhat reminiscent of the old cyclist in a regional stage of the Tour de France. He competes every year and the locals wait for him to pass the finishing line – but he never does, according to the writer.

Beckett's record of bravery during the Second World War is well documented. He acted as a messenger and translator of news on the 'free radio stations'. He belonged to the Resistance cell called 'Gloria'. There were one hundred members but only twenty-three survived. Like many foreigners, he came under the suspicion of the Gestapo. They called to his apartment but left, placated, when they spotted a copy of *Mein Kampf* on a bookshelf. He played down his involvement with the Resistance, calling it 'boy scout stuff'. However, Free France disagreed and awarded him the Crois de Guerre (with a citation signed by Charles De Gaulle).

Most of the characters in the Beckett landscape hobble about, often without purpose, in a futile attempt to pass the time. They are often old, decrepit, and diseased. Voices raised in anguish... failures. For Beckett it was important to struggle on: 'Ever tried. Ever failed. No matter. Try again. Fail again. Fail better'.

He achieved most recognition for his plays, notably *Waiting for Godot* (1948–49), *Endgame* (1957), *Krapp's Last Tape* (1959) and *Happy Days* (1961). He died in 1989 and is buried in Montparnasse cemetery. A lone tree stands at the foot of his grave.

TRINITY COLLEGE – 'CRADLE OF GENIUS'

THE BUILDING that overshadows Dublin is the fortress-like Trinity College. Joyce described it as 'the grey block of Trinity set heavily in the city's ignorance'. He was on his way to the Catholic University on St Stephen's Green and may not have appreciated the rectangular beauty of what is the oldest university in Ireland. The college was founded in 1592, about a quarter of a mile southeast of the city walls of Dublin. The area now covers some 40 acres of cobbled squares and green spaces, and houses a collection of architectural riches that date back three centuries.

Queen Elizabeth wanted to establish a college of 'the most holy trinity' and set about finding the right place for it. She chose an old Augustinian Abbey that had been suppressed in 1538, tore it down, and built a college for the teaching of Divinity to the young Protestant gentlemen of the region. She was concerned about the effects of the Counter Reformation in Ireland, so she built a wooden structure in Dublin 'whereby knowledge and civility might be increased by the instruction of our people there, whereof many have heretofore used to travail into ffrance, Italy and Spain…whereby they have been infected with poperie and other ill qualities and soe become evil subjects'.

Students were known to be at their desks at 6.30 in the morning. Prayer meetings and sermons in Latin were followed by mandatory visits to the cathedrals of Christ Church and St Patrick. But there ended the piety. From then on into the night it was 'town versus gown' and the young bloods of Trinity introduced a new raucousness to the streets and taverns. They were often to be seen rioting, playing dice, insulting women, and boozing and bawding in the alehouses nearby.

Narcissus Marsh was the Provost of Trinity when he became Archbishop of Dublin in 1689. A scholar and linguist, he introduced the study of Irish to Trinity. He also gave his name to one of the great libraries of the city. Early readers were 'graduates and gentlemen' and they were locked into reading cubicles with rod and chain.

Catholics were admitted to Trinity until the early seventeenth century, but they were banned from attending the college during the Penal Laws (which were modelled on those enacted against Huguenots in France). The Catholic Relief Act of 1793 allowed them back. In 1944, however, Archbishop McQuaid announced that Catholics should not go to Trinity because of its Anglican orientation. He warned that if they did so, the sacraments would be denied to them. This threat was ignored by many non-conforming Catholics; in the 1960s, the 'ban' was honoured on paper more than in reality.

In 1969, the college debating society (the Phil) had to amend its rules of membership. The often quoted maxim 'only when a man walks on the moon shall women be allowed into this society' had to be revoked. Women had entered the college as undergraduates in 1904, against the express wishes of the Provost Salmon. 'Over my dead body', he said, in the year that he passed away.

The Long Room, Trinity

© Fáilte Ireland

Famous literary alumni of Trinity include Jonathan Swift, Oliver Goldsmith, John Millington Synge, Oscar Wilde, Edward Carson, Abraham Stoker, Eavan Boland, Brendan Kennelly, Sarah Berkeley, Vona Groarke and Paula Meehan. In 1969, Samuel Beckett followed the physicist Ernest Walton in winning a Nobel Prize (Walton had won in 1951). He did not attend the ceremony in Stockholm and, always publicity-shy, reacted negatively to the announcement that he had won: 'It's a disaster', he told his partner, Susanne.

Beckett on his Alma Mater: 'Trinity is full of the cream of Ireland, rich and thick'.

BRENDAN BEHAN (1923–1964)

An author's first duty is to let down his country

HELLRAISER AND dramatist Brendan Behan was born into a fiercely Republican family. One of his uncles, Peadar Kearney, wrote the Irish national anthem, *Amhrán na BhFiann,* and many of the clan had taken part in the 1916 Rising. Like many Irish writers, he had a love/hate relationship with the country of his birth. 'I regard Ireland in the same way as Sean O'Casey', he said. 'It's a great country to get a letter from'. His relations with Church and State were stormy. In the 1940s, he was excommunicated by the Irish hierarchy for his activities with the IRA and got to know the Irish penal system at first hand. It compared unfavourably with its English counterpart: 'If you ever want to go to gaol, I recommend an English one', he said.

Prison life was the closest Behan got to a formal education. His two best works, *Borstal Boy* and *The Quare Fellow,* draw vividly from his experience of life on the inside. He travelled widely – Paris, New York and Toronto – following productions of his plays. Behan had a nose for self-publicity, which did not harm the box office. He played the stage Irishman abroad, raising the roof wherever he went and puncturing any pompous questions about his plays. One journalist asked him, 'What message is in your plays?' Behan replied, 'What do you think I am, a feckin' telegraph pole?'

The 'roaring boy' pulled in an entourage wherever he went. When Behan arrived in New York in 1958, 'it was dead' (according to Norman Mailer) but 'Behan made the beatnik generation popular uptown'. His play *The Hostage* was running off Broadway and his autobiographical novel *Borstal Boy* had just been published. People were curious about this Irish phenomenon and expected a memorable quote to every question. Behan did not disappoint them. When he was asked to define the difference between prose and poetry, Behan paused and reportedly came up with this gem of doggerel:

© Failte Ireland

There was a young fella called Rollocks,
Who worked for Ferrier Pollocks,
He walked on the strand,
With his girl be the hand,
And the tide came up to his...knees

'Now that's prose. If the tide had come any higher, that would've been poetry'.

Alcohol destroyed Brendan Behan's talent. He was often picked up by the New York police, having been found wandering the streets of the city. He even spent some time in the New Jersey State Psychiatric Hospital. Behan returned to Ireland and spent his last months with family in his native Dublin. In the Bailey pub on Duke Street, friends waited for news of his death. When the inevitable day came (in March 1964), Flann O'Brien remarked: 'The streets of Dublin are strangely silent tonight'.

Typical of his legendary wit (some would say apocryphal wit) Behan could manage a last quip, even in his hospital bed. An old nun was tending the ailing writer in his last hours. He thanked her devilishly: 'God bless you sister. May you be the mother of a bishop'.

EAVAN BOLAND

Poetry begins where the certainties end

EAVAN BOLAND was born in 1944. Her mother, Frances Kelly, was an artist and her father was a diplomat. Much of her early life was spent abroad. She was educated in New York and London, and she graduated from Trinity College with a first in English literature. In her twenties, she covered poetry readings for the *Irish Times* and remarked upon how valuable it was to hear other poets reading. She liked to hear a poem read for the first time – its first take. A reader's power and passion were important to her. Painters influenced her too – she liked how they waited for the light to be just right before beginning.

Boland's first poem was seen in print when she was just seventeen, and her first collection was published when she was twenty two. She married in her mid-twenties and moved to the suburbs of south Dublin, which placed her outside the governing body of male poets. Her life in the enclosed world of suburbia comes through in her work. Observations about those quiet moments, watching her young children develop – and the 'folklore behind the net curtains' – have gained her a wide readership in Ireland and America. The toxins of Irish history are also source of inspiration to her. The poem *Quarantine* is a heartbreaking account of a man and woman's struggle to survive in the worst year of the Great Famine. For Boland, the Irish past is filled with 'shadows, silence and furtive whispers'.

She is often referred to as Ireland's premier 'female poet', and she likes the label. She is a feminist but not a feminist poet. Unlike Yeats, she does not feel the need to comment or posture about the

Ireland she lives in. She feels her duty is done when she creates a good poem.

Eavan Boland's *New Collected Poems* was published in 2006. She teaches at Stanford University in the United States.

CON HOULIHAN

The George Best of the written word

Stephen McMahon

KERRY-BORN Con Houlihan is perhaps the last surviving journalist of the old school of pub writers. The inscription on a bust in his hometown of Castleisland describes him as a fisherman, turf-cutter, rugby player and teacher. He asked that the word 'lover' be left out.

One of his earliest influences was the writer and teacher Daniel Corkery, who Houlihan remembers saying: 'When man goes to the moon how will people react? They will think more and more about their own little parish'. Con Houlihan replaced his small parish of Castleisland in north Kerry with another in Dublin: Burgh Quay. His beloved *Irish Press* was published there until 1995. The 'Press' had an envied reputation for sports coverage – particularly of Gaelic football and hurling. Con Houlihan made himself into a household name by reporting on the games that were played in every parish in Ireland. He stood among the fans on the terraces, rather than in the press box. However, sports journalism was not his first assignment. David Marcus, the literary editor of the *Irish Press*, sent him a copy of Solzhenitsyn's *The First Circle* to review. He recalled that when his by-line appeared in the *Irish Press*, it was like being elected captain of the local rugby team.

Burgh Quay had shops, bookmakers and several pubs, but no brothel. In his view, it therefore did not qualify as a proper village in the French sense. Local pubs like Mulligan's, the Pearl, the White Horse and the Silver Swan (affectionately known as the Mucky Duck) were all frequented by journalists and literary folk. Houlihan avoided the quasi-intelligentsia in McDaid's. He admired Flann O'Brien's prose and Patrick Kavanagh's poetry but otherwise kept a discrete distance.

If you walk along the canal by Rathmines Bridge, you might catch a glimpse of a gargantuan figure with flowing grey hair and a hand shyly covering his mouth as he stops to speak to a friend or stranger – that is Con Houlihan.

More Than A Game, a selection of his essays on sport, was published in 2003.

SEAMUS HEANEY (1939–)

A great poem is deeper than its declared meaning

SEAMUS HEANEY was the eldest of nine children in a Catholic farming family from County Derry. He won a scholarship to St Columba's College (a boarding school) in Derry and then took a first at Queen's University in 1961. In 1972, he left his lecturing job at Queen's and came to live in Glanmore in County Wicklow. He had decided to 'put the practice of poetry more deliberately at the centre' of his life.

When asked about his inspiration, he said that poems came from 'remembered things...little bleepers' during periods of incubation, like on long car journeys when 'driving with the spouse is stilling'. Planes and hotel rooms were also creative places, as one is cut off. He pointed out that the best poems are those completed quickly. He shared Coleridge's view that poems that were dwelled on too long were 'like schoolboys that grew dull from too much correction'.

He eagerly began writing poetry in 1962, when he was twenty three. There was 'plenty of charge in the battery' then. Patrick Kavanagh, who also came from a farming family, was a major influence on his work. The troubles in Northern Ireland erupted as he began publishing his work and, like Bob Dylan, he was roundly criticised for not being the spokesman for his constituency. Instead, he drew on mythology and ancient history to comment on the politics of the day. Memories of his parents are a rich and happy vein. Poems like *Mossbawn Sunlight* (from the collection *North*) and *Digging* (from *Death of a Naturalist*) are in praise of them. Grief and sadness are also represented in his work: *Mid-Term Break* is a poignant poem about the death of his four-year-old brother in a car crash.

He began guest lecturing at American universities, and he has been the Boylston Professor of Rhetoric and Oratory at Harvard since 1984. Robert Lowell regarded him as the 'most important Irish poet since Yeats', and he has triggered the phenomenon known as Heaney-bopping because of his worldwide popularity. In 2003, he took the unusual step of praising the 'verbal energy' of the rapper Eminem – he said the singer had sent a 'voltage around a generation'. The compliment would help him to reach a whole new audience of poetry readers.

Preoccupations (1968–1978) – a selection of his prose – is an ideal introduction to Ireland's most recent Nobel Laureate.

JAMES JOYCE (1882–1941)

When I die Dublin will be written in my heart

JAMES JOYCE was born in Dublin in 1882, to an affluent family from Cork City. His father, John Joyce, was feckless: drinking by profession and impoverishing the family before the young Joyce went to live in Zurich and Trieste in 1904. He was twenty two years old and already convinced of his impending greatness. He was not going to bend the knee: 'I will not serve that which I no longer believe, whether it calls itself my home, my fatherland or my church'.

Joyce feared that the forces of catholicism and nationalism would throw nets over his soul and stifle his creativity, so he got out. He rarely returned, although he did toy with some entrepreneurial ideas of running a cinema and exporting Irish tweed and linen to Italy. His first work of prose was *Dubliners* (1904). *A Portrait of the Artist as a Young Man* was published in America in 1916. It was quickly recognised as a masterpiece; as the story of an Irish Catholic upbringing, it has not been equalled.

He was educated by the Jesuits at Clongowes Wood College in County Kildare and at Belvedere College in Dublin. Father Conmee was the rector and he offered to have the gifted youngster educated at Belvedere for free. Joyce's father jumped at the suggestion. At least his son would not suffer the indignity of an education along with 'Paddy Stink and Micky Mud' at a Christian Brothers school. Joyce was grateful for his Jesuit education; it taught him how to 'order and how to judge'.

During the First World War, he worked on *Ulysses* (which was published in 1922). In this book, he immortalises not only himself but also the city of his youth. The novel deals with eighteen hours in the life of the city, using many literary styles, allusions, and the vernacular language of Dubliners to create an intricate mosaic of life in one place. His feel for the external sound and tangled appearance of the city was faultless, but what made the book revolutionary was his understanding of the inner consciousness of his characters.

It took Joyce seven years to write *Ulysses* (it took this writer seven years to read it). Joyce joked that he wanted to keep the academics busy for a century. How right he was! Joyce has become an industry for academic interpretation. Controversy has followed his name in publishing circles throughout the world. Even the Irish writer Roddy Doyle got in on the act recently, when he declared: 'Joyce needed a good editor'. Yeats described the book as 'the vulgarity of a single Dublin day prolonged to 700 pages'.

Many enthusiasts believe that *Ulysses* should be read aloud and in a Dublin accent. Brendan Behan thought it was a 'good gag book'. W.B. Yeats could not understand it, but Joyce had predicted as much when he met the poet on his way to Paris. On hearing that Yeats had turned forty, Joyce remarked: 'You are too old for me to teach'.

The world may have been ill prepared for *Ulysses*, but it had to wait more than sixteen years for Joyce's great puzzle, *Finnegans Wake* (1939). The book is set in the dreaming sub-conscious of a Chapelizod publican named Tim Finnegan. In this 'book of the night' Joyce pushed language to its limits. He literally wrote a new language – some called it gibberish. Nonetheless, the book gave him tremendous pleasure to write. His wife, Nora, recalls being woken one morning by the sound of her husband laughing out loud at something he had just written. 'Jim, either stop writing or stop laughing', she shouted. The book is packed with historical anecdotes, popular ballads, old Dublin jokes and scandals, and almost anything else that took Joyce's fancy at the time.

James Joyce died in Zurich in 1941. The atmosphere of the Swiss city reminded him of his hometown. Coincidentally, his first landlady in Zurich was a Frau Dubliner. Joyce was amused. He never lost interest in his native city, and there was a constant stream of visitors from Ireland. It seems he had softened his attitude to his fellow countrymen in later years, when he declared: 'The Irish are the most intelligent, most spiritual and most civilized people in Europe'. This is quite a turnaround from another statement: 'Ireland is the old sow that eats her farrow'.

PATRICK KAVANAGH (1904–1967)

IN 1939, Patrick Kavanagh – the 'peasant poet' – arrived in Dublin, the city that he often despised. He was the son of a cobbler and small farmer from County Monaghan. The rural mannerisms of this sensitive soul were to earn him the cruel mockery of the city's literary community. Tall and thin, with horn-rimmed glasses and a floppy hat, he cut a conspicuous figure, muttering to himself as he walked to the bookmakers and the pubs of the town.

When Kavanagh moved to Dublin he became a freelance journalist, writing reviews for the *Irish Times*. The work brought him into contact with the intellectual set of the Palace Bar in Fleet Street. He was not impressed. He viewed them as the dregs of the old literary revival but entered their orbit for conversation and to make valuable contacts. He worked regularly for the *Irish Press*, and wrote a twice-weekly gossip column under the *nom de plume* of Piers Plowman. When Yeats died in 1939, Kavanagh set out to obtain the mantle of Ireland's premier poet. Indeed, he felt that the Anglo-Irish as represented by Yeats were not qualified to speak about the real experience of Irishness.

One part of the Dublin that he haunted was Baggot Street, a delightful avenue of fine Victorian redbrick buildings. He was a regular in two pubs along the street: the Waterloo House and Searson's (Searson comes from the old Norse *Sigurson*).

The area was to become his 'Pembrokeshire', gradually becoming his village away from home. It had a cast of the usual 'irregulars'. Everything that aided civilized living – a few pubs, a bookshop and a bookmakers – was there. He wrote eloquently about the area in his verse. He took solace from the Grand Canal – the statue, known as the 'crank on the bank' commemorates the many hours he spent there, contemplating the water falling 'niagarously' towards Dublin Bay.

'Let words laugh', Kavanagh once wrote. One of his most famous poems, *Raglan Road*, was set to an ancient Irish air, *The Dawning of the Day*. It tells the bittersweet story of his love for a young girl (later to marry

O commemorate me where there is water – Patrick Kavanagh   © Failte Ireland

Donagh O'Malley, a government minister). The song became hugely popular. It has been sung by many notable musicians, including Van Morrison, Billy Bragg, Sinéad O'Connor and, most memorably, Luke Kelly of the Dubliners.

Much of Kavanagh's work saluted the mundane in everyone's parish: the canal, the back lane, the street or the cutaway bog. Seamus Heaney, an early disciple, said that Kavanagh sought to 'register the unregarded data of the usual life'. Kavanagh influenced almost all of the current generation of poets. When they entered the pubs in the 1960s and listened to the mix of information, gossip and malice, he appeared to be exempt from (routine) scathing criticism.

Poverty saved Kavanagh from habitual drinking. When his income became modest, though, he drank heavily: from 1960 until his untimely death in November 1967.

PAULA MEEHAN (1955–)

THIS DIMINUTIVE writer was born on the northside of the city and grew up in the working class suburb of Finglas. She took the escalator to Trinity College, eventually becoming a writer-in-residence there. At the same time, she worked with prisoners in Mountjoy Gaol; it was from this work that her stage play *Cell* emerged.

Among her influences was the writer and Trinity lecturer Brendan Kennelly, who told her that behind every piece of writing was a human life. Her grandfather turned her into 'a print junkie' by teaching her to read before she went to primary school.

Meehan's work and use of the vernacular (Dublinese) comes from her strong working class roots, where the mother figure is a formidable 'warrior' against poverty and social discrimination. It is small wonder that her work is deeply autobiographical and lionises her mother's and her grandmother's strength and courage.

For Meehan, poetry is about public performance. Unlike many poets, she is an excellent reader of her work. Connecting with the community remains important to her; she does not want to appear as an isolated academic force. She teaches creative writing in schools and community groups. In her readings for TV and radio, her spirited intellect comes across through her strong voice. Although she has trouble thinking of poetry writing as a career, she brings it to the centre by making her poems accessible to the non-specialist reader. Like her mother, she is a warrior for her times.

FLANN O'BRIEN (1910–1966)

FLANN O'BRIEN (real name Brian O'Nolan), from Strabane in County Tyrone, is probably Ireland's best-known satirical writer of the twentieth century. He was educated at University College Dublin, where he studied English, German and Irish. He became something of a celebrity in the university debating society, where many of the country's lawyers and politicians first cut their teeth. His wit and skill in deflating the phoney legalism and mock-sophistication of the society were legendary.

When he finished his MA, he applied to the Irish Civil Service and was appointed to one of only three positions that were available. He successfully completed his probation in 1937, having learnt how to write dreary memos and curb his acerbic tongue. Like many other artists, actors and literary folk who also worked in the Civil Service, he felt imprisoned by the institution. However, he was 'a straight by day and a swinger by night'.

A series of bogus letters to the editor of the *Irish Times*, which drummed up mock controversies for readers, brought him to the attention of Bertie Smyllie (who was then the editor). The back room of the Palace Bar often acted as the editor's office. Smyllie would proceed through the public bar to the 'intensive care unit' at the rear. He would place his hat on the seat beside him and allow anyone to occupy that spot and make a pitch.

Smyllie spotted O'Brien's talent but was nervous about his anarchic tendencies. When he took over as editor, he wanted to broaden the appeal of the newspaper, and take it away from its West British worldview. What better way than to employ one of the most brilliant satirists to write a bilingual column. English was not O'Brien's first language. He spoke Irish until the age of six. Indeed, his father did not want his sons educated in the English language at all.

He began work on *At Swim Two Birds* (his first novel) while still at university; it was published by Longman's in 1939. Graham Greene was the reader. He said he experienced 'the kind of glee one enjoys when people smash china on stage' and thought it 'one of the best books of the century'. All but 250 copies were destroyed during the Blitz in London. O'Brien sent a copy to James Joyce, who had escaped to Paris. His reaction was pleasing: 'That's a real writer, with a true comic spirit…a really funny book'. Dylan Thomas read the book and declared: 'This is just the book to give your sister if she is a loud, dirty, boozy girl'. Joyce encouraged O'Brien to promote the novel on mainland Europe. Sadly, though, Joyce died in 1941, before he could be of any further help to the younger writer.

Flann O'Brien is probably best known for his column in the *Irish Times* – An Cruiskeen Lawn ('little brimming cup'). The articles were written under the name of Myles na Gopaleen (Myles of the Little Horses) and they gained him a wider audience than many of his works of fiction did. These short bursts of satirical fire were often written in one sitting. The column was supposed to be penned in Irish but O'Brien reverted to English (sometimes even German and Latin) and poured scorn across a range of subjects, including the Plain People of Ireland, The Brother, and The Catechism of Cliché. When too drunk to deliver copy he would bring a drinking companion to the pub to write down his musings on the folly of Irish life – or even on how to turn Guinness into solid cubes. He said that you could suck on one of these cubes to alleviate the boredom of being dragged to Sunday Mass by the spouse.

Although his pseudonym protected Flann O'Brien from exposure within the Civil Service, his anonymity did not last. He was 'retired' from the service on health grounds – the combination of alcoholic writer and unhinged satirist was too dangerous to handle. There is an often repeated story about when his superiors finally challenged him about his excessive drinking during office hours: 'You were seen coming out of the Scotch House at 2.30pm', they said. He replied, 'You mean I was seen coming in'.

SEAN O'CASEY (1880–1964)

> ...the bare bones of a fanlight
> Over a hungry door...

> Louis MacNiece

UNLIKE MOST of his contemporaries, Sean O'Casey was born into a poor Protestant family, who lived in the north inner city slums of Dublin. He suffered from bad eyesight from an early age but, as he said, 'it didn't matter, because there was nothing much to look at anyway'.

For many years, he lived at home with his mother and worked as a labourer. He was self-educated, reading Shakespeare and the plays of Dion Boucicault (he even appeared in one of his dramas). O'Casey became involved in the labour movement and the Dublin 'Lock Out' of 1913 but he quarrelled with James Larkin and later with the leaders of the 1916 Rebellion. For him, there was no brotherhood between nationalist and socialist.

His first play was rejected by the Abbey Theatre in 1919 but the *Shadow of a Gunman* premiered there in 1923. His masterpiece, *Juno and the Paycock*, was produced the following year. Women were often the central characters and the life force in his plays – they were the people of action, while male figures postured and strutted about like peacocks boasting about their own past. *Juno and the Paycock* was a huge critical success, and it saved the Abbey from certain bankruptcy. *The Plough and the Stars*

© Failte Ireland

followed quickly, as did the most dramatic riot since Synge's *Playboy of the Western World*. The realistic depiction of the Easter Rising – with the looting of shops, the revolutionary flag being seen in a pub, and an Irish woman being portrayed as a prostitute – were not acceptable to those Irish Nationalists who saw the play. They even sang the national anthem from the theatre's balcony as an artistic riposte.

This trilogy of plays and six autobiographies form the cornerstone of O'Casey's reputation as a writer. He never regained the critical success of those early years and chose to live abroad after the Abbey rejected his anti-war play, *The Silver Tassie*, in 1928. He later said, 'It takes both courage and patience to live in Ireland'. He settled in Torquay, Devon and lived there until his death in 1964.

GEORGE BERNARD SHAW

(1856–1950)

I am a typical Irishman; my family came from Yorkshire

GEORGE BERNARD Shaw — dramatist, critic and pamphleteer — was born in Synge Street in and grew up there in genteel poverty.

© Failte Ireland

His mother was Lucinda Gurly, sixteen years younger than her husband, George Shaw, an unsuccessful grain merchant and serious drinker. Bernard Shaw (he hated the name George) began working as a junior clerk at the age of fifteen and followed his mother to London when she went there to teach music. He left Dublin when he was twenty, calling it 'a city of slack-jawed blackguards'. He did not return for almost thirty years, thereafter preferring annual trips to County Cork and County Kerry until 1923. His father had died in 1885; none of the family attended his funeral. Shaw was deeply patriotic about his Irish roots. He once remarked: 'Whenever Londoners ask me the meaning of those dreadful words Sinn Féin, I tell them it is the Irish for John Bull'.

Shaw began his career as a music critic, having bolstered his education at the British Museum. He joined the socialist Fabian Society in 1884 and became the champion of many causes, including feminism, vegetarianism, the abolition of private property, and even the simplification of the English alphabet. He was a lifelong teetotaller and non-smoker (something of a record for an Irish writer).

He attacked capitalism and war in his plays and essays. His anti-war pronouncements made him unpopular during the Great War; theatres refused to stage his plays because he was deemed unpatriotic. He remained unbowed and continued to be a prolific writer. Indeed, he was often described as the 'second Shakespeare'. Like the Bard, he came under the hammer of the British censor when his play *Mrs Warren's Profession* was banned.

After 1918, war veterans flocked to see his plays, knowing he had told the truth about the war. Arguably, his most famous work is *St Joan*, which was written three years after she was declared a saint. *Pygmalion* became the hugely successful film *My Fair Lady* (starring Audrey Hepburn as Eliza and Rex Harrison as the irascible Professor Higgins). Shaw was awarded the Nobel Prize for Literature in 1925; he is one of three Dublin writers to be given the honour.

In 1898, he married Charlotte Payne-Townshend, a woman of independent means. However, he carried on platonic affairs, usually by letter, with other notable women of the age, including Mrs Patrick Campbell and the actress Ellen Terry. Bernard Shaw wrote over fifty plays, many of them 'comedies of ideas'. He continued to write into his nineties. He died in Ayot St Lawrence in 1950.

JOHN MILLINGTON SYNGE
(1871–1909)

THIS GREAT dramatist was born to a well-to-do landowning family in south County Dublin. He once said that he did not have a proper conversation until he was in his twenties. The life of the Anglo-Irish drawing room salon left him cold. He responded more to the mist and light winds of the Wicklow Mountains, where he wandered alone, stopping at the doorways of peasant farmers and conversing with them in their native tongue. His fluency in Irish was to open up a world hitherto unknown to him or other members of his class. Synge soon understood the richness of the Irish language as spoken by the peasant, a language that had been ignored by the dominant culture.

Like many other writers and artists, Synge spent time in Paris. Perhaps they all responded to Gertrude Stein's view that 'Paris *is* the twentieth century'. Synge met James Joyce when he was on his way home from studying music in Augsburg, Germany. Joyce recalled his 'harsh gargoyle face'. Synge also met Yeats in Paris. Yeats said: 'Give up Paris. You will learn nothing by reading Racine. Go to the Aran Islands. Live there as if you were one of the people themselves. Express a life that never before has found expression'. It was to be a decisive moment for the young dramatist. Yeats had put his finger on something. Until the turn of the twentieth century, the Irishman was portrayed onstage as a small man wearing a cap, carrying a stick, and perhaps holding a pig under his arm. Women fared worse: Caitlín Ní Houlihán was seen outside a thatched cottage churning butter and lilting an Irish air.

© Failte Ireland

The characters in Synge's plays were portrayed quite differently. They used vivid language to express themselves; it was the Irish vernacular translated into English. They were proud of their place and their deeds. The hero of the *Playboy of the Western World* boasts about killing his father. He stands outside the rule of law that applied in the Pale. The sexual longing of Pegeen and Christy, the central characters, was expressed clearly in the *Playboy* (which was unusual for the time).

When the play arrived in Dublin, nationalists could not handle this new portrayal of Irishness. Riots broke out at the first production in the Abbey Theatre in 1907. In Philadelphia, the whole company was arrested for indecency. In court, a lawyer asked an eyewitness, 'Did anything immoral happen onstage?' 'Not while the curtain was up', came the reply.

Synge's plays were often attacked as 'pseudo Irish'. The *Irish Times* said that *Riders to the Sea* (1904) was 'quite unfit for presentation on the stage'. The play is now recognized as a brilliantly constructed one-act play about death. Synge was the first truly Irish playwright. All other Anglo-Irish writers had written mainly for an English audience and either ignored or distorted Irish affairs to please audiences in Drury Lane or the Haymarket. Synge wrote solely for his own people: the impoverished Irish peasant. He was quite indifferent to the criticism and controversy surrounding his plays. With a shrug worthy of Gary Cooper, he just rolled another cigarette and handed it to one of the actors.

JONATHAN SWIFT (1667–1745)

JONATHAN SWIFT was born beside St Werburgh's Church in 1667. He was educated at Kilkenny Grammar School and came to Trinity College at the age of fifteen. Like many other Protestants, he fled the country for England during the Jacobite wars in 1689, returning to 'wretched Dublin in miserable Ireland' in 1714. He then spent a brief spell in County Antrim. He became chaplain to Lord Berkeley in 1699 and Dean of St Patrick's in 1713. He considered the position to be a form of banishment.

Swift's Deanery was in the heart of the Liberties, in the city centre. Certain inherited privileges came with the job, one of which was to give sanctuary to fugitives. The people he ruled were the impoverished who lived in the five acres of his parish. He came to identify with this underclass, walking among them and emptying his pockets of coins as he passed by. Swift readily took up the economic plight of the poor, becoming a champion of an early 'Buy Irish' campaign, when the

© Failte Ireland

Huguenot manufacturers of silk and wool could not sell their produce in England.

All around Swift, the line between poverty and great wealth was becoming more defined. Vainglorious monuments were erected to the greatness of men who had saved Ireland for Protestantism. For example, in 1701, great pomp and ceremony surrounded the unveiling of a statue of King William of Orange, who defeated the Jacobean army of James I at the Battle of the Boyne in 1691. The statue was often attacked (beheaded or defaced), not so much by the resentful Catholic mob but more by the students of Trinity College, who took offence to William sitting with his back to their venerable seat of learning. The IRA tried to blow up the statue in 1929 but it was a botched effort. The Dublin wags noted that the explosion had caused the heroic William to turn from king into queen!

In one of Swift's most celebrated literary outings he adopted the pseudonym of M. B. Drapier to expose the granting of a patent that would allow a private individual to mint inferior coins for use in

Ireland. The resulting seven letters became a *cause célèbre* and led to a £300 reward being offered for the identity of the writer. Nobody squealed, and the action that the government took against the publisher collapsed when the jury refused to return a guilty verdict. Swift became a national hero and was given the freedom of the city of Dublin in 1729.

For Swift, satire was 'a sort of glass, wherein beholders do generally discover everybody's face but their own'. His best-known send-up was called *A Modest Proposal*, in which he recommends that poor children should be cooked and served as food at the tables of the rich. He writes:

> *I have been assured by a very knowing American of my acquaintance in London, that a young healthy child well nursed is at a year old a most delicious, nourishing, and wholesome food, whether it is stewed, roasted, baked or boiled; and I make no doubt that it will equally serve in a fricassee or a ragout.*

The full version was read aloud by Peter O'Toole at a glittering gala to reopen Dublin's Gaiety Theatre in 1984. Much to his amusement, the actor was booed off the stage by the assembled *haute bourgeoisie*.

Swift often gave pertinent advice, especially to old men: 'Never marry a young woman'. To him, the best doctors in the world were 'Doctor Diet, Doctor Quiet and Doctor Merryman'. Swift's private life invited much speculation. He was deeply attached to two women: Esther Johnson and Esther Vanhomrigh (whom he nicknamed Vanessa). Swift's self-penned epitaph was considered by Yeats to be the 'greatest in history':

> *Swift has sailed into his rest;*
> *Savage indignation there*
> *Cannot lacerate his breast.*
> *Imitate him if you dare,*
> *World-besotted traveller; he*
> *Served human liberty.*

OSCAR WILDE (1 8 5 4 – 1 9 0 0)

No man is rich enough to buy back his past

OSCAR WILDE'S background was unconventional. His mother broke with her Unionist roots and became immoderate in her sense of style, wearing increasingly outlandish head-dresses bedecked with bizarre jewellery. Her poetry was inflammatory. Dubliners applauded her when she walked along the street after writing seditious editorials for *The Nation*. She was devoted to her second son, Oscar, and he to her. He once wrote: 'Where there is no extravagance there is no love, and where there is no love there is no understanding'. She would leave Dublin and move her salon to London to be near him.

Wilde was a student of the Classics at Trinity. However, after just two years there, he won a scholarship to Magdalen College, Oxford. John Pentland Mahaffy, his tutor, broke the news: 'You're not quite clever enough for us here, Oscar. Better run up to Oxford'. When word got out that Wilde was leaving Dublin, the wags remarked: 'Poor Oscar. He'll have no competition over there'. He spent four years at Magdalen; he graduated in 1878, 'a formed man'.

The frock coat worn by men represented the formal constraints of the Victorian age. Wilde discarded it in favour of his own sartorial style and became a dandy. He took to wearing tweed jackets with large check patterns, tall collars and curly brimmed hats. His sexuality at this time was equivocal. Wilde was engaged to Florence Balcombe for a time, but she ended the relationship and married his fellow Trinity College student Bram Stoker.

His high-spending lifestyle in London led him to do what many educated men of the time did to pay off creditors: a lecture tour of America. Art and Aesthetics were his two chosen topics. The silver miners of Leadville in Colorado turned up to hear him speak:

> *I spoke to these delightful fellows about the early schools of Florentine painting, and they slept as peacefully as if no crime had ever stained the ravines of their*

mountain homes. I described to them the pictures of Botticelli and the name which sounded to them like a newly invented drink roused them from their slumbers. I read them passages from the autobiography of that great Florentine genius and adventurer Benvenuto Cellini and he proved so popular he that they asked as one man 'why the hell I hadn't brought him with me'. I explained that Benvenuto had been dead for some years which elicited the immediate demand: 'who shot him'.

© Fáilte Ireland

Afterwards, they invited me to supper and, having accepted, I had to descend a mine in a rickety bucket in which it was impossible, even for me, to remain graceful. At the bottom of the mine we sat down to our banquet: the first course being whiskey, the second whiskey and the third, whiskey. The amazement of the miners when they saw that art and appetite could go hand in hand knew no bounds, and when at last I lit a long cigar and quaffed a couple of cocktails without flinching, they cheered me until the silver fell in a glittering dust from the roof onto our table below.

His greatest triumph was the stage play *The Importance of Being Earnest*, which was produced in 1895. His curtain speech was vintage Wilde. He declared that the play was already a great success. He thanked the audience for being such a success too, and noted that they regarded his play almost as highly as he did himself. The *New York Times* wrote:

'Oscar Wilde may be said to have at last, and by a single stroke, put his enemies under his feet'. How wrong this judgement turned out to be!

The gladiatorial battle about his sexuality drew as much laughter in court as his plays did on stage. A fellow Trinity student, Edward Carson QC, cross-examined Wilde:

> CARSON: Do you drink champagne yourself?
>
> WILDE: Yes. Iced champagne is a favourite drink of mine — strongly against my doctor's orders.
>
> CARSON: Never mind your doctor's orders sir!
>
> WILDE: I never do.

Nonetheless, the trials were to be the end of Oscar Wilde. He had cocked his nose at the Victorian establishment once too often, and he had picked the Marquis of Queensbury — an 'infamous brute' — as a most formidable enemy.

He died in Paris in 1900. He had become a tainted figure of public scorn. Many people were afraid to sit with him at the boulevard cafes of Paris. The novelist André Gide sat with his back to the street for fear of being recognised beside the disgraced Irishman. Wilde beckoned Gide to sit alongside him. 'I am so alone these days', he said.

SALONS AND CLUBS

THE DUBLINERS' gift for words made them the 'greatest talkers since the Greeks' and the literary salon was where they sharpened their wit. Because the city was so small, everybody worth knowing could be found in either the salon or the pub.

One of the best-known Dublin salons was started by George A. E. Russell (1867–1935). At the turn of the twentieth century, this 'big bearded' poet, mystic and artist opened his home on Rathgar Avenue to new literary talent. They were dubbed Russell's 'poultry yard' or his 'canaries'. Sunday was the day on which he allowed guests to talk and eat his cherry cake. He published three of Joyce's stories from *Dubliners* in the *Irish Homestead* (known also as the 'Pig's Paper'). Yeats's wife called A. E. a saint. 'You [Yeats] are a better poet but no saint'. The dramatist Sean O'Casey was not impressed by 'the spate of blather' at A.E.'s and attended only twice.

Entertaining at home flourished at the beginning of the twentieth century. The poet Padraig Colum and his wife, Mary, entertained every person of importance in the city. She found Dublin to be full of 'intelligence and nimble wits' and they came to her house on Tuesday evenings.

Daly's was a notorious house that opened on College Green in 1791. It was once described as the 'most superb gambling house in the world'. The club began as a chocolate house but the change of use and proximity to Parliament and Trinity College ensured a brisker trade in the 'flutter'. The sumptuous club, designed by Francis Johnston, traded night and day. In the afternoons, the blinds were drawn and the chandeliers lit to effect a continuous nocturnal atmosphere. The buck and the rake idled away their time here, and then disappeared into what is now Temple Bar to sample the pleasures that it offered at the turn of the nineteenth century.

In the early twentieth century, high society was served by eight gentlemen's clubs. The Stephen's Green Club – originally a town residence – was at number 9. After the Act of Union was passed, the house was let out as a garrison for £150 a year. The oldest and most famous gentlemen's club was the staunchly unionist Kildare Street Club, which was founded in 1782. In 1897, Edward Martyn – bankroller of the Irish Literary Theatre and co-founder of the Feis Cheoil (Festival of Music) – entertained priests and republicans in the club's lounge, much to the annoyance of Unionist members. The writer George Moore noted that he was 'neckless as an owl'. Martyn was expelled from the club for objecting to Edward VII's visit in 1907.

Moore, in *Parnell and His Island*, recalled the atmosphere and the type of men who assembled in the Kildare Street Club:

> [The club] represents those who are gifted with an oyster-like capacity for
> understanding this one thing: that they should continue to get fat in the

bed into which they were born...there they remain spending their days drinking sherry and cursing Gladstone. (Gladstone introduced the first Home Rule Bill for Ireland in 1886.)

By the end of the 1950s, the modern generation of writers was being well served by a salon at 11 Lad Lane. It was run by the short-story writer Mary Lavin, who welcomed new writers, including Seamus Heaney, Paul Durcan, Thomas Kilroy and John McGahern. They knew there was a good chance they would meet older, more established, authors like Frank O'Connor and Patrick Kavanagh. The Mews was to become Lavin's *Dead Poets' Society*. It was both 'cave and castle upholstered in Irish tweed'. The door policy was 'open house' and so nobody needed an invitation to enter. The atmosphere was distinctly bohemian in 'the sweep of hair, scarf, cloth and those good shoes' that she liked to see people wear.

WILLIAM BUTLER YEATS

(1865–1939)

W. B. YEATS was a man born to controversy. Family evenings were alive with argument about the state of politics, art and society. The poet's father, John, pronounced lucidly on all of these matters. William reached out to a world of the imagination and the spirit to satisfy his thirst for truth. His father helped there: he believed the boy was getting on too well at the High School in Rathgar and sent him to art school instead. From an early age, Yeats became deeply attached to the west of Ireland, staying with his granmother Susan Mary Pollexfen in County Sligo, and exploring the world of Celtic fairy lore and old Irish mythology. He also became fascinated by the occult.

The poet had aristocratic links with the Ormond family, which may have influenced his character and demeanour. He used his autocratic nature at timely intervals, especially when he took to the

Abbey Theatre stage to quell the riots on the far side of the footlights. There was no one better suited than Yeats to take on the backward elements of a society that wished to blunt the intellectual freedom of 'his' literary movement. He co-founded the national theatre in 1904, and discovered John Millington Synge and Sean O'Casey, who were to become two of the country's most famous dramatists; he would cross swords with anyone who dared to silence them.

Yeats wrote verse from an early age. His introduction to the visual arts made him determined to pursue a literary career. In 1892, he founded the National Literary Society, which he used to promote an independent view of Irishness: proud, heroic and in touch with its Celtic roots. He always returned to the spiritual and mystical in his work. His stage play *Caitlín Ní Houlihán* was first produced at the turn of the century. It had a huge influence on those who saw it. Some years later, Yeats said: 'Did that play of mine send out certain men the English shot'? Indeed, it did. An old woman comes onstage and mourns the loss of her 'four green fields'. She wonders if any young man will help her to win them back. The significance of the play was not lost on Patrick Pearse, one of the leaders of the 1916 Rising. Yeats was to pay tribute to him and all that 'delirium of the brave' in the poem *Easter 1916*, when he declared, 'A terrible beauty is born'.

Many saw Yeats as a traitor to his class, and the doors of Anglo Ireland were shut coldly in his face. Nonetheless, there was always refuge with Lady Gregory in Coole Park. It was there, in his beloved West of Ireland, that he could find food for thought and much needed food for his belly.

The novelist and playwright Kate O'Brien recalls seeing Yeats as he progressed along St Stephen's Green from Maud Gonne's house:

> *Yeats looked magnificent. He was tall and heavy and he strode head in air, chanting and talking to himself. The head was heavy, the heavy hair fell back from it; the ribbon fluttered from the eye-glasses, the fur-collared coat flapped open...he always carried books and papers; he always walked as if through empty space.*

My Ireland

Yeats was awarded the Nobel Prize for Literature in 1923 and was a senator of the Irish Free State until 1928. His last decade proved to be his most creative. He experimented with drugs to revitalise himself physically and was energised enough to produce three of his best volumes: *The Tower*, *The Winding Stair* and *Last Poems*. He died in 1939, and was finally laid to rest in Drumcliff, County Sligo. He chose his own epitaph: 'Cast a cold eye on life, on death, horseman, pass by'.

THE MONTO APRÈS CLOSING TIME

FOR A long time, Dublin had soldiers garrisoned inside and outside its walls. At the beginning of the nineteenth century, though, the will to suppress Irish rebellion took on a new vigour. From the time of Robert Emmet's aborted revolt in 1803 to when British regiments returned from the Crimean War, the city was full of soldiers – and vice. One side of O'Connell Street became known as the respectable side when prostitutes began to promenade on the opposite pathway.

It was the 'Monto' – named after Montgomery Street, which was within walking distance of the city's docks – that earned the *Irish Times* headline 'a loathsome locality'. From the 1880s onwards brothels (known as 'kip houses') were confined to this area. Up to 1,600 women worked there at any given time. Many were in debt and in fear of the ferocious madams who ran these premises.

There were brothels to suit every taste. 'Flash' houses catered for the upper end of the market, including army officers. When a new regiment came to town, welcome cards were sent to the officers' mess. The ladies would take a carriage out to race meetings and be followed back to the Monto by parties of lusty gentlemen (including Edward VII in 1907). In the house of the infamous Mrs Mack (85 Mecklenburg Street), girls like Becky Cooper and Fleury Crawford wore evening dress and burned coal instead of turf in the grate.

After the Defence of the Realm Act in 1916, brothels served alcohol when pubs were closed, and this led to a surge in business. Joyce sketches the atmosphere of the Monto in the 'Nighttown' chapter of *Ulysses*: Bloom enters the area and is subjected to a sequence of hallucinatory events and grotesque appearances from his subconscious. In *A Portrait of the Artist as a Young Man*, the young Joyce is lured by the sound as much as by the scent of the girls from the Monto. The writer recorded some of their mating calls:

> *Hello Bertie, any good in your mind? Is that you pigeon? Good night husband! Coming in to have a short time? Fresh Nelly is waiting for you.*

The boom in the Monto continued to match the howl of the guns during the Great War. By 1917, there were 132 brothels and 1,700 working girls. But change was coming. The new Puritanism of the Irish Free State, allied to the foundation of the Legion of Mary, along with Jesuit support, exploded one night in March 1925. The police rampaged through the area, arresting over 100 people. A religious procession followed and brought many girls to their knees as it passed. The zealots stopped at each brothel to pin a holy picture above the door. It was the end the road for the Monto.

Beckett, Samuel. *A Beckett Reader*. New York 1976

Behan, Brendan. *Borstal Boy*. London 1956

Bennett, Douglas. *Dublin Anthology*

Boland, Eavan. *Selected Poems*. Pennsylvania 1989

Boland, Eavan. *Object Lessons*. Manchester 1995

Bowen, Elisabeth. *Seven Winters*. Dublin 1942

Brown, Christie. *Down all the Days*. London 1970

Clerkin, Paul. *Dublin Street Names*. Dublin 2001

Craig, Maurice. *Dublin 1660-1860*. Dublin 1980

Cronin, Anthony. *Dead as Doornails*. Dublin 1976

Cronin, Anthony. *No Laughing Matter: A Biography of Flann O'Brien*. London 1989

Cronin, Anthony. *The Last Modernist*. London 1996

Donleavy, J.P. *The Ginger Man*. Paris 1955

Donoghue, Emma. *Stir Fry*. Dublin 1994

Duffy, Noel & Dorgan, Theo. *Watching the River Flow: A Century in Irish Poetry*. Dublin 1999

Ellmann, Richard. *Four Dubliners* London 1987

Ellmann, Richard. *James Joyce*. New York 1982

Ellmann, Richard. *Yeats — The Man and the Mask*. London 1979

Fitch, Noel Riley. *Sylvia Beach and the Lost Generation*. New York 1985

Gray, Tony. *Mr Smyllie*, Sir. Dublin, 1994

Heaney, Seamus. *Preoccupations: Selected Prose 1968-1978*. London 1980

Houlihan, Con. *More than a Game*. Dublin 2003

Igoe, Vivien. *James Joyce's Dublin Houses*. London 1990

Joyce, James. *A Portrait of the Artist as a Young Man*. New York 1916

Joyce, James. *Ulysses*. London 1960

Kavanagh, Patrick. *Collected Poems*. London 2004

Kearns, Kevin, C. *Dublin Pub Life and Lore*. Dublin 1996

Kelly, Deirdre. *Four Roads to Dublin*. Dublin 1995

Kiberd, Declan. *Inventing Ireland*. London 1995

Levenson, Leah. *The Four Seasons of Mary Lavin*. Dublin 1998

Lyons, F.S.L. *Ireland Since The Famine*. London 1971

Maddox, Brenda. *Nora*. Boston 1988

Magee, Malachy. *1,000 Years of Irish Whiskey*. Dublin 1980

McCann, Sean. *The Story of the Abbey Theatre*. London 1967

McDonald, Frank. *The Destruction of Dublin*. Dublin 1985

Molloy, Cian. *The Story of the Irish Pub*. Dublin 2002

Montgomery Hyde, H. *Famous Trials: Oscar Wilde*. London 1962

Moore, George. *Hail and Farewell*. London 1911

Murray, James. *Classic Irish Whiskey*. London 1997

Nicholson, Robert. *The Ulysses Guide*. London 1988

O'Brien, Edna. *The Country Girls*. London 1960

O'Brien, Kate. *My Ireland*. London 1937

O'Casey, Sean. *The Plough and the Stars.* London 1932

O'Connor, Ulick. *All the Olympians*. New York 1984

O'Connor, Ulick. *Brendan Behan*. London 1970

Pakenham, Thomas & Valerie. *Dublin: A Travellers' Companion*. London 1988

Ryan, John. *Remembering How We Stood*. Dublin 1975

Somerville-Large, Peter. *Dublin*. London 1979

Stephens, James. *The Insurrection in Dublin*. Dublin 1916

Swift, Jonathan. *A Modest Proposal*. Dublin 1729

Thom's Official Directory. Dublin. 1870, 1882, 1904, 1916, 1922, 1930, 1940, 1950.

Tucker, Bernard. *Jonathan Swift*. Dublin 1983

Yeats, W.B. *Collected Poems*. London 1990

WEBSITES:

Ireland.com

Wikipedia.com

Post.ie

Independent.ie

WHAT THE PRESS SAID ABOUT
THE DUBLIN LITERARY PUB CRAWL TOUR

"This is the most ingenious crash course in Irish literature, history, architecture and pub bonhomie yet devised… It combines street theatre with the 'craic' that makes Dublin pubs the liveliest in Europe and successfully avoids the clichés that would otherwise ruin an evening of high art and low life."
THE TIMES (London)

"A highly enjoyable evening that gives you the pleasant notion of replacing brain cells as you drown them."
IN DUBLIN

"Excellent! This is by far the most entertaining way to get a real feel for the city's booze-fuelled literary heritage."
EYEWITNESS GUIDE BOOK

"This is no ordinary tour. Those who book it are transported away from the aridity of the tourist clichés to the richness of the language of Joyce, O'Casey, Yeats and Behan."
TORONTO STAR

THE DUBLIN LITERARY PUB CRAWL

STARTING POINT: The Duke pub, 9 Duke St.,

SUMMER: Every evening at 7.30pm *(April – October)*
WINTER: *(Nov-March)* Thursday, Friday & Saturday 7.30pm.
Sundays *(all year)*: 12 noon & 7.30pm

Further information call 353 (0)1 670 5602
353 (0)87 263 0270

www.dublinpubcrawl.com